HOW TO TALK CONFIDENTLY WITH YOUR CHILD ABOUT SEX

Lenore Buth

Parents'
Guide

This second edition was formerly titled *Sexuality: God's Precious Gift to Parents and Children* in the Concordia Sex Education Series published in 1982.

Book Six of the Learning about Sex Series

The titles in the series:

Book 1: Why Boys and Girls Are Different
Book 2: Where Do Babies Come From?
Book 3: How You Are Changing
Book 4: Sex and the New You
Book 5: Love, Sex, and God
Book 6: How to Talk Confidently
         with Your Child about Sex

Developed under the auspices of the Family Life Department, Board for Parish Services, The Lutheran Church—Missouri Synod.

Scripture quotations marked TEV are from the Good News Bible, the Bible in TODAY'S ENGLISH VERSION. Copyright © American Bible Society 1966, 1971, 1976. Used by permission.

Scripture quotations marked NEB are from THE NEW ENGLISH BIBLE (NEB) © The Delegates of The Oxford University Press and the Syndics of the Cambridge University Press, 1961, 1970, and are used by permission.

Scripture quotations marked Phillips are from J. B. Phillips: THE NEW TESTAMENT IN MODERN ENGLISH. Revised Edition © J. B. Phillips 1958, 1960, 1972. Used by permission of Macmillan Publishing Co., Inc.

Scripture quotations marked KJV are from the King James or Authorized Version of the Bible.

Scripture quotations marked RSV are from the Revised Standard Version of the Bible, copyrighted 1946, 1952 © 1971, 1973. Used by permission.

Scripture quotations marked NIV are from The Holy Bible: NEW INTERNATIONAL VERSION, © 1973, 1978, 1984 by the International Bible Society. Used by permission of Zondervan Bible Publishers.

Illustrations by Maritz Communications Company. 1988 cover design by Concordia Publishing House.

Copyright © 1982, 1988
Concordia Publishing House, 3558 South Jefferson Avenue, St. Louis, Missouri 63118

MANUFACTURED IN THE UNITED STATES OF AMERICA

  2   3   4   5   6   7   8   9   10   97 96 95 94 93 92 91 90 89

Contents

Editor's Foreword

This book is one of a series of six published under the auspices of the Board for Parish Services of The Lutheran Church—Missouri Synod through its family life department.

Originally published in 1982, the series was updated in 1988. To indicate more precisely that it's a *sex*-education series, all books were given new titles and cover designs. Books four through six were expanded to include topics of current concern such as the sexually transmitted diseases AIDS and chlamydia.

Books in the series are (former titles in parentheses): *Why Boys and Girls Are Different* (*Each One Specially*) (Ages 3–5); *Where Do Babies Come From?* (*I Wonder Why*) (Ages 6–8); *How You Are Changing* (*How You Got to Be You*) (Ages 8–11); *Sex and the New You* (*The New You*) (Ages 11–14); *Love, Sex, and God* (*Lord of Life, Lord of Me*) (Age 14+); and *How to Talk Confidently with Your Child about Sex* (*Sexuality: God's Precious Gift to Parents and Children*).

The last book in the series is designed for adults, to help them deal with their own sexuality, as well as provide practical assistance for married and single parents in their role as sex educators in the home.

Like its predecessor, the new *Learning about Sex* series provides information about the social-psychological and physiological aspects of human sexuality. But more: it does so from a distinctively Christian point of view, in the context of our relationship to the God who created us and redeemed us in Jesus Christ.

The series presents sex as another good gift from God which is to be used responsibly.

Each book in the series is graded—in vocabulary and in the amount of information it provides. It answers the questions that persons at each age level typically ask.

Because children vary widely in their growth rates and interest levels, parents and other concerned adults will want to preview each book in the series, directing the child to the next graded book when he or she is ready for it.

In addition to reading each book, you can use them as starting points for casual conversation and when answering other questions a child might have.

This book, or parts of it, can also be used for discussion in an adult class, a parents class, or a parent-teacher group. There is also a videocassette which may be used in a discussion session with adults. The videocassette depicts sexual development and ways in which parents and other concerned adults may help their growing children develop healthy, Christian attitudes about their sexuality.

Frederick J. Hofmeister, M.D., FACOG, Wauwatosa, Wisconsin, served as medical adviser for the series. Rev. Ronald W. Brusius, secretary of family life education, Board for Parish Services, served as chief subject matter consultant.

In addition to the staffs of the Board for Parish Services and Concordia Publishing House, the following special consultants helped conceptualize the series: Darlene Armbruster, board member, National Lutheran Parent-Teacher League; Betty Brusius, executive director, National Lutheran Parent-Teacher League; Margaret Gaulke, elementary school guidance counselor; Priscilla Henkelman, early childhood specialist; Rev. Lee Hovel, youth specialist; Robert G. Miles, Lutheran Child and Family Service of Michigan; Margaret Noettl, family life specialist; and Rev. Prof. Rex Spicer, D.Min., family life consultant.

Rev. Earl H. Gaulke, Ph.D.

Introduction

So God created man in His own image; in the image of God He created him; male and female He created them. . . . And God saw all that He had made, and it was very good.

Genesis 1:27, 31 NEB

This is a book about that three-letter word:

S—E—X.

Sex has gone from being a subject decent people did not mention, to one that permeates every facet of our lives: the movies and television shows we (and our children) watch, the comic strips and books we read, the songs we sing and the jokes which bring a laugh, the clothing we wear and the weight we watch, the constant commercial advertisements for everything from "feminine products" and cosmetics to cigars and tractor tires. In short, even if we wanted to we couldn't escape the fact!

We are sexual beings! And that's the way God created us—male and female. We are distinctly different. And alike.

What shaped us most as we grew up were the attitudes and values we caught from our parents. In the words of the old saying, "The apple does not fall far from the tree." As our children, in turn, absorb our attitudes about sexuality, they also assimilate our hang-ups and misconceptions.

Thus one of the purposes of this book is to help you deal with your own adult sexuality. If you are married, it will aid you in enjoying a warm, mutually satisfying relationship. If you are single, it will help you better understand your own sexuality. In either case, coming to terms with your own sexuality provides a solid foundation for your children—a healthy pattern for them to follow.

As part of the Learning about Sex series, this book is also meant to be a guide for married and single parents. As such it gives practical assistance so you can guide your children in dealing with their own sexuality and adopting God-pleasing values. Only then can they wisely use God's precious gift.

This book is about sexuality and it's about relationships—husband and wife, parents and children. It's about attitudes—those we've acquired along the way and those we hope to instill in our children. And it's about freedom—the freedom God has given us to see our bodies and our sexuality as He meant them to be when He created that first man and woman:

Behold, they are very good!

1. *Sex and Sexuality Are Not the Same. Or Are They?*

Thou it was who didst fashion my inward parts;
Thou didst knit me together in my mother's womb.
I will praise Thee, for Thou dost fill me with awe;
wonderful Thou art, and wonderful Thy works.
Thou knowest me through and through:
my body is no mystery to Thee.

Psalm 139:13-15 NEB

When a child is born, mother, father, doctor, and nurses all want to see for themselves whether the baby is male or female. They determine this, of course, by noting the child's genitals. Friends and relatives ask, "Is it a boy or a girl?" because most of us still carry preconceived ideas about what having a child of either sex will mean. In that context "sex" means the child will likely play with either dolls or toy trucks, will grow up to be a nurse or a fireman—and eventually a mother or a father, if parenthood is the person's choice.

The word "sex" is also commonly used to mean sexual intercourse. "So and so are having sex." "It's so bad at home that my husband and I haven't had sex for weeks." "My children learned all about sex at school."

But sex is more than gender, more than sexual intercourse, more than "sex education." Sex is not what we *do*, but what we *are*. Actually a better term would be "sexuality," for our being male or female influences every aspect of our lives.

Sexuality means more than a woman dressing in a feminine manner or a fellow who's a "real he-man type." It's more than preferring fashion and love stories to tearing down cars and football games. Sexuality encompasses our attitudes, our strengths and weaknesses, our whole way of looking at life. It includes such culturally determined characteristics as:

—the name we were given at birth
—the toys we played with as children
—whether we chose home economics and typing in high school or woodworking and machine shop
—whether we identified with Romeo or Juliet, with Tarzan or with Jane
—whether we felt more comfortable preparing a financial report or decorating a room.

All these and more are acceptable social customs. As such they are mostly *learned* rather than just a part of being one sex or the other. For years there have been "normal" roles for either male or female, but that is changing rapidly. The shift is good, of course, if it keeps us from putting each other—and our children—into stereotypes.

However, that same change has made it more difficult for many of us to determine just what's expected of a man or a woman. For instance, having all types of careers open to both sexes is exciting; the prospects are limitless. On the other hand, young people may think they "should" do something out-of-the-ordinary. A young woman may believe she "should" try out for the police force when she'd really rather be a top-notch secretary.

MALE AND FEMALE: ALIKE OR DIFFERENT?

Besides the cultural customs that have conditioned us, there are the biological differences. Yes, there *are* differences, although the lines are not so clearly drawn as they once were thought to be. It can't be denied that males have greater physical strength in most cases, although females generally have more endurance. For example, females can tolerate the cold for longer periods of time because they have a larger percentage of body fat (which acts as insulation) than males do, even when at their ideal weight.

Men and women often display differing attitudes as well. For generations it was assumed that women were more sensitive, more tender, had more protective feelings toward their children. Men were thought to be work-centered, aggressive, and largely incapable of

8

deep emotions or sensitivity. Today we know those differences are mostly conditioned during childhood.

For example:

* Little girls are hugged and comforted when they cry.
* Small boys are told, "Only babies cry. You're a little man, and men don't cry!"
* Girls are taught to be "nice," to be "little ladies."
* Boys are encouraged to be tough; when they get in trouble, parents fondly remark, "Boys will be boys!"
* Girls play tea party.
* Boys play with trucks.

The result of this trying to live up to the "acceptable" image is really rather sad. Many grown men, for instance, repress their tender feelings and wouldn't think of crying, fearing they will appear weak. Many women with a natural aptitude for science choose instead to go into teaching English, then wonder why they're not satisfied with their work. A husband may be terrible with figures and the wife a whiz, yet both may think that he, as head of the house, "should" handle the finances. A father may think caring for their child is "the mother's job," thereby missing out on the joy of getting to really know his youngster.

Today those old roles are becoming blurred. Women are doctors, lawyers, mechanics, farmers, and firefighters, to name a few. Men are nurses, gourmet cooks, social workers, and nursery school teachers. There are successful marriages where the wife earns the living for the family while the husband stays home, caring for the children and keeping house. Men—and women—are becoming aware that a man who can cry is, in fact, strong—secure enough to realize his manhood does not hinge on a carefully maintained mask.

Most of us probably think we're quite modern in our thinking, yet we may find such changes hard to accept. But who's to judge what's "right" if these people are fulfilled in their work or their roles? For today more and more people, especially the young, believe people should do what fits them. Nevertheless, it still takes a strong sense of self-identity to go against accepted customs.

SELF-IDENTITY IS IMPORTANT

It is important to know who you are as a person. That means a male can be confident enough in his masculinity to be gentle and tender, to share his fears, to do "woman's work" if he chooses—without apology or embarrassment. It means a female can be a telephone line worker or a mechanic without feeling she has lost her femininity. Inside ourselves we know we are male or female, no matter what work we choose.

Liking ourselves is also part of self-identity. When we can accept ourselves as redeemed children of God, we can be secure in our relationships. It's not really complicated. The more we see our own worth as a person, the more we have to give to a marriage. "For many years I tried to be what I thought Steve wanted me to be," Dana said. "Steve's never been much for art, so I packed away my easel and paints and tried to learn to like sports, as he does. But I just couldn't get interested.

"As time went by I began to resent all the time and money we devoted to *his* pleasures while I never even got near my paint brush. I blamed Steve for that and after awhile our relationship was in bad shape. As for sex . . . we might as well have slept in separate rooms.

"One day I decided I'd had it. I stormed into the den and said, 'Steve, I'm going to take a painting class this fall and I don't care what you say!' He looked at me in amazement and said, 'Well sure, Hon; I've been wondering when you'd start painting again.'

"Then I realized it had been my fault all along, " Dana said sheepishly. "Steve just figured if I'd wanted to paint, I would have. So now I'm taking classes and turning out paintings. Some please me, some don't. But the important thing is that I feel good about *me*. And you know what? Steve has a new look in his eyes, too. Call it respect if you like. For the first time in years I recognize my own worth, and it's made all the difference in our relationship. Sex? Well, it's never been better!"

Dana and Steve learned what many couples have found to be true. Respecting each other's differentness, appreciating each other's contribution to the marriage, enjoying our own and our partner's sexuality enable us to be truly free and secure with each other. That kind of base provides a firm foundation for a lifetime of growing together. And separately. This is the bedrock for a relationship—sexual or otherwise—in which both partners can function fully.

THE SEXUAL RELATIONSHIP—MORE THAN INTERCOURSE

The sexual relationship between husband and wife is not simply two partners who engage in sexual intercourse. Rather a couple's sexual relationship also reflects the way they act toward each other in other areas of their life. That's not surprising, for the marital sexual relationship involves the union of our minds and emotions as well as our bodies. It's a "total" relationship.

Our ongoing best efforts are required to achieve that oneness. The result makes it well worth our time and trouble. Mutual support and closeness become an all-day feeling and help both husband and wife to feel close when they shut their bedroom door.

Yet no relationship is forever the same. No two days, no two years are identical. "Sometimes I feel so close to Warren," said Linda. "But there are other times when we're getting along but we're not close. As for sex, sometimes the only description is wonderful. Other times it's just sort of so-so. Is everyone like us?"

These are normal variations. We're human beings and as such are not stamped out of a press. Each of us is unique, always changing. And our relationship is a living thing also, rather than settled into a fixed format.

NURTURING THE RELATIONSHIP

All living things need nourishment. A close, happy marriage requires love, commitment, empathy, communication, and respect if it's to continue growing. It also requires reinforcement by being with other stable couples who are committed to making their marriages thrive. (For if we continually associate with those who trumpet the advantages of "me first"—rather than giving first place to their marriage relationship—or of "swinging," extramarital affairs, divorce, and "single bliss," it will be much more difficult to view our own marriage in a positive light. Those negative attitudes will inevitably rub off on us.)

We can give support to other couples, too. Our own good relationship can serve as an example for others. We do have a stake in the marriages of others. Each time a union fails, our own sense of the permanence of marriage erodes a bit.

Christian couples, pledged to making their relationships blossom, can be a powerful witness in the world. They can exemplify what God intends marriage to be: the union of two people in a lifelong commitment to serve each other, growing as individuals and as a couple, and living in love.

Also of concern to us parents is our example to our own children. As they grow up they're constantly learning about life. Each day they add another piece to the jigsaw puzzle, trying to get a complete picture of how to relate as male or female, as a marriage partner, as a parent. We portray that picture as we relate to each other—and to them.

2. In the Beginning Were Male and Female

And so the Lord God put the man into a trance, and while he slept, He took one of his ribs and closed the flesh over the place. The Lord God then built up the rib, which He had taken out of the man, into a woman. He brought her to the man, and the man said:

'Now this, at last—
bone from my bones,
flesh from my flesh!—
this shall be called woman,
for from man was this taken.'

That is why a man leaves his father and mother and is united to his wife, and the two become one flesh.

Genesis 2:21-24 NEB

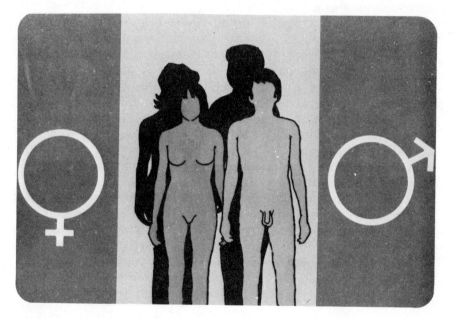

When God created human beings He made two complementary sexes, male and female. The word "rib" could be translated "side"; in that context, woman is the other side of man.

In marriage, which God ordained, man and woman have ample time and opportunity to discover how they complement each other. In most marriages spouses are interdependent; one partner's weak point may well be the other's strength. In one marriage the husband will be a good money manager while the wife wants no part of handling family finances. In another marriage the husband will say, "My paycheck burns a hole in my pocket, so now I just turn it over to my wife. Our finances run much more smoothly when she pays the bills and gives me pocket money."

These natural differences simply illustrate again that we're not rolled off an assembly line. Rather each of us is a unique creation of God—one of a kind. In the same way each marriage relationship is singular, not to be measured against another marriage.

As stated in the Introduction, the most important thing we can do for our children (and ourselves!) is to keep our husband-and-wife relationship thriving. You've probably experienced it yourself—if you feel close and loving, everything else seems better too.

"It's really silly!" says Lynn with a laugh. "When things are going well between Alec and me I can handle anything. The car can break down, the washer can flood, the kids can come down with measles, but I can take it in stride. I know that underneath all that our relationship is solid and everything else is just temporary.

"But there are other times—we call them our gray days—when we feel apart, when we've stopped communicating. At times like that our sexual relationship usually suffers from the blahs too. Life seems dull and empty—one long round of hard work and being taken for granted. The future looks like endless years of more of the same and I wonder 'How did I get myself into this?' At those times I don't feel I can cope with *anything!* Then finally we turn the corner and begin to feel close again."

IS THERE ROMANCE AFTER MARRIAGE?

Most of us who've been married for some time realize that every marriage has its ups and downs, so we hang on and wait for things to get better as experience has proved they will. But even in the best of marriages we're probably well aware there's been a deterioration in the romance department. What romance, you ask?

Before marriage she made herself as attractive as possible whenever she would be seeing her love. She was willing to go to football games, on fishing trips and mountain hikes. It didn't matter that she might dislike these activities. They were an excuse to spend time with the one she loved, and no sacrifice was too great. She also complimented him often on how strong he was, how good-looking, how all-around marvelous.

For his part, he wooed his beloved with flowers, candy, dinners, the theater, movies, concerts, art galleries, etc. All she had to do was mention something she'd like to do, for her wish was his command. And he delighted in telling her how beautiful she was, how sweet, how desirable.

"And then we were married," complains Marlene. "Now I can't get him inside an art gallery or near a concert, and the only time he brings me flowers is when I have a baby! As for compliments, forget it! He never notices how I look. And I can work all day fixing a good meal which he wolfs down without a word. Then he plunks himself down in front of the TV for the evening. If I try to carry on a conversation he gets mad and says, 'Sh! Can't you wait for a commercial?' "

"For Pete's sake!" exclaims Hank. "What does she expect? She should know I consider her attractive and my kind of woman. I married her, didn't I? Of course when she drags around the house in that old bathrobe, with no makeup and straggly hair, she's not exactly the same gal I married!

"As for going places, what about Marlene? She won't go to a football game with me, either. Of course I watch TV. And as for compliments, well, she doesn't exactly flood *me* with them, either. Instead I hear, 'Can't you ever remember to hang up your clothes?' or 'Don't you think you could use a shave?' or—silliest of all—'Won't you *please* learn to put the lid down on the toilet?' In case Marlene hasn't figured it out, that kind of talk doesn't give me romantic thoughts!"

Sustaining courtship levels of romance is, of course, impossible over the long haul, when immersed in the routine of making a living and raising a family. All of us take each other for granted after a time. (And that's not *all* bad, for it's inevitably one element in feeling secure with our marriage partner.) Where once we talked endlessly, as if there would never be enough time to share all the feelings inside, now we may have run out of subject matter. Our conversation may center around such exciting topics as "Did you pay the phone bill?" and "Be sure to check the tire pressure next time you fill up the car with gas."

But how do you keep romance alive when you have clamoring kids and a limited budget?

"Blake and I had drifted into a bad pattern. We didn't even get each other birthday gifts," says Dee Ann. "We told ourselves we didn't need 'all that foolishness.' Our marriage had become downright boring, even though we still loved each other. So we decided to put forth some effort to make things interesting. We couldn't afford babysitters and big nights out, so we realized we'd have to use our ingenuity.

"Now at least once a week I put the kids to bed early, set the table with our best china, and fix a special dinner. We light candles and have soft music in the background with lots of time to just sit and talk and dream together. It's something we both look forward to!" says Dee Ann, her eyes shining.

"We write love notes to each other, too—just short and simple like 'I can't wait until we're together' or 'You are God's gift to me' or something like that. I put them in Blake's lunch or tape one to the dashboard of his car or stick one in his pocket—someplace where he'll find it when I'm not around. He hides notes for me, too. Or we put up

14

signs for each other. Some people might laugh, but it means a lot to us.

"It's fun to get each other unexpected gifts and little treats, also. When I go shopping I may pick up a special snack Blake loves. Sometimes I buy a magazine he never gets for himself. Or when I take the kids to the library I look for a book Blake would like.

"He enjoys surprising me, too," continues Dee Ann with a smile. "The best thing is when he gives me a 'gift certificate' of time. For instance, he'll promise to watch the kids and run errands on Saturday so I can have the day to myself. And sometimes I do the same for Blake—like getting everybody out of the house so he can relax and watch a TV football game in peace. None of these things cost much or take much effort—but it means a lot to realize the other person took time and thought in a busy day to let you know you're loved. Believe me, it's made a world of difference in our marriage!"

THE REWARDS MAKE IT WORTH THE TROUBLE

Most of us have the habit of thinking of expensive gifts or outings, so our loving gestures are limited in number. Actually the small things often mean the most. As Dee Ann and Blake discovered, all it requires is thoughtfulness and a bit of creative thinking. The result of feeling loved is that we respond more enthusiastically in our daily life and in our sexual relationship.

Many couples enjoy sending their children off to the grandparents for an occasional weekend. Or they may arrange to exchange baby-sitting with another couple. During the weekend they may take a short trip, check into an area hotel, or just spend the time doing something they'd never do otherwise. Perhaps they might choose to stay home and sleep late in the morning, with uninterrupted opportunity to talk, to caress, to have sexual intercourse if they choose.

Consider declaring your bedroom off-limits to problems with the children, business worries, or other nagging concerns. That room should be a haven where husband and wife concentrate on each other.

"I always wondered why Barry and I felt so romantic on vacation— but only on vacation," says Irene. "It was almost like flipping a switch! We immediately became as we were on our honeymoon. We made love frequently, were constantly touching. All those wonderful, warm feelings came over us in a flood and we felt like two youngsters! Then we'd go home, vowing to hang onto our new closeness—and quickly be right back where we were before! There we'd be lying side by side in our own bed, talking about the children and the business and how to make the money stretch. Feeling nothing.

"But then I heard a marriage counselor on television say that couples should watch what they talk about in their bedroom. So we decided to give it a try. It took a while to break our old habits, but it has really made a difference. Now when I walk into the bedroom I

15

remember all the love we've shared there. It's become a very special place for both Barry and me. We close our door and shut out the world for a little while."

THINK AHEAD

It's a good idea, too, to *schedule* some time alone on a regular basis. Some husbands and wives have a "date" every week or two, so they can look forward to it when life seems humdrum.

Al and Marty, for instance, have a standing date for breakfast every Wednesday. "It's the highlight of my week," says Marty. "Al works weekends but he has Wednesday mornings off. We get the kids off to school and then go out for a leisurely breakfast at a nice restaurant—and we can because breakfast is the least expensive meal to eat out. It's a real treat to be alone with Al. It's about the only time we get a chance to finish a sentence!"

Keeping the marriage relationship fresh and alive does require some effort, but it's energy well spent!

DON'T STOP TOUCHING

Study a young couple newly in love; they seem compelled to be touching almost constantly. By contrast a pair who has been married for some time may seldom touch each other except during sexual play and intercourse. In fact, sometimes one or both partners avoid touching deliberately, fearing it may lead to sexual intercourse.

The truth is we all need touching, all through our lives. Studies show that babies and young children deprived of touching and cuddling fail to develop normally. Touch is a vital part of our communication as marriage partners, too—one which benefits both. When touching is a frequent, natural part of the relationship, there's never a reaction of "She's only pawing me because she wants something" or "He ignores me all day and then expects me to turn on the minute we shut the bedroom door."

"Jerry comes from a family that never showed affection," says Ellen, sighing, "while my family is always touching—and hugging and kissing. When we were dating, Jerry would kiss me goodnight and that was about it, but I thought he was just keeping his distance until we were married. I soon found out I was wrong! The only time he came near me was when he wanted sex. When I complained that he never showed he loved me, he'd say, 'That's a stupid thing to say! I come right home every night and I'm faithful to you. What more do you want?'

"I finally realized that Jerry really wasn't comfortable touching people. Even me. So I decided I'd have to take the initiative," Ellen continues. "First I found a time to talk when I was sure he'd listen and I explained how much it meant to me—that to me touching means love. And I told him I intended to keep on touching *him*, whether he appeared to notice or not, because *I* needed it. Pretty soon Jerry began to like having me come up and hug him and kiss him. Now he often makes the first move. In fact I think he'd miss it as much as I!"

COMMUNICATION: WHAT IS IT?

All couples need communication—by touching and by talking about their feelings, their needs, their hopes and dreams. Good communication is the basis for everything else. Even sex. Of course it's possible for a couple to have a good sexual relationship without communicating in other ways, but it's rare.

Communication means more than just talking. Over the years many couples drift into a pattern of small talk—surface-level conversation. But in true spirit-to-spirit communication we're free to share our deepest feelings, both good and bad, with our partner.

"I can tell Mickey anything," says Debbie. "I know he's the one person in all the world who accepts me as I am, even though he knows all about me. He respects my right to be a separate person, too, and he cares about my hurts as well as my triumphs. And I know I can trust him all the way. He'd never put me down or laugh at me. He'd never knowingly embarrass me, and he wouldn't take something I confided in him and use it against me later. I guess the best thing about Mickey is that I can always count on him to support me and try to understand. And I try to do the same."

That's marriage as God would have it.

Suppose a couple has drifted into a relationship where there's an invisible wall between them, dating from a time when one said or did something the other just can't forget. Maybe one or both are afraid to take off their self-protective masks. They *want* to keep each other at a distance because there's less chance of being hurt. Or possibly the couple has never experienced more than occasional moments of feeling close.

What then?

CAN PEOPLE CHANGE?

"Frank and I had been married a long time," said Charlotte, "but our marriage was nothing to brag about. He went his way, and I went mine. We didn't have much to talk about but our two children.

"Then our adult Bible class at church studied marriage. We began to see that marriage was meant to be more—much more. At first we couldn't even talk about the deadness in our relationship. It hurt too much," says Charlotte wistfully. "We *did* love each other, though, so after a few weeks we began to open up a little. But I kept remembering that old saying, 'Can a leopard change its spots?'

After awhile our class discussion got around to the power available to Christians—how Christ's love enables us to sweep aside the past and forget old hurts. They even had a Bible verse for it. I memorized it because I needed to say it over and over to myself:

If any man be in Christ, he is a new creature; old things are passed away; behold, all things are become new.

2 Corinthians 5:17 KJV

"Frank and I decided that promise was meant for us, too, and we would make a new start in our marriage, depending on God to heal old wounds and make us 'new creatures.' We began with small things—like setting aside a half hour for a cup of tea and talk every night before bedtime. At first we felt awkward—couldn't think what to say!

"Before long we really started to talk—and to understand each other," said Charlotte, eyes glowing. "I guess the change really came when we got up the courage to pray together. Now our relationship is so much closer I can hardly believe we're the same people. On the other hand, maybe we're not! The funny thing is that our sex life has improved, too. Before, Frank and I were almost like brother and sister. Now . . . well, let's just say we're more like newlyweds!"

It bears repeating: Good communication is the basis for a good relationship, both sexual and otherwise.

3. The Sexual Relationship: Ordained by God

> Be faithful to your own wife and give your love to her alone. . . . Be happy with your wife and find your joy with the girl you married. . . . Let her charms keep you happy; let her surround you with her love.
> Proverbs 5:15, 18-19 TEV

Sexual intercourse between a male and a female is often said to be "doin' what comes natch'rally." In a sense that's correct. The act of mating requires only two bodies, two sexes, two sets of genitals. It can be merely a chance encounter, a moment of passion, the fulfillment of a biological urge.

But the continuing marital sexual relationship is something totally different. It was ordained by God. He designed our bodies to give and receive pleasure with each other. Our sexual natures are a *gift* from God—to be enjoyed without shame or embarrassment. Although that seems a simple truth, we often allow it to become complicated.

"It's surprising to hear the misconceptions people have," says one pastor. "When couples come to me for counseling, they often have sexual problems. For instance, some use sexual intercourse as a sort of reward for good behavior. If their partner makes them angry, they refuse intercourse.

"Then there are the couples who say to me, 'Pastor, it's sinful to enjoy sex too much or to have relations too often. As Christians we should set our minds on higher things!' My reply is always the same—that God's Word doesn't bear that out.

"Of course," continues the pastor, "that's not to say a marriage without sex is wrong—if both partners are happy with the arrangement. But I believe God meant husbands and wives to express their love for each other freely—in many ways, including sexual intercourse."

KNOWING OUR OWN BODIES

Marriage is meant to be the lifelong union of two persons. We've already focused on the importance of love and communication between husband and wife as the prime factor in a good sexual relationship. But it can also be helpful to look at the miracle of our bodies and of how they function.

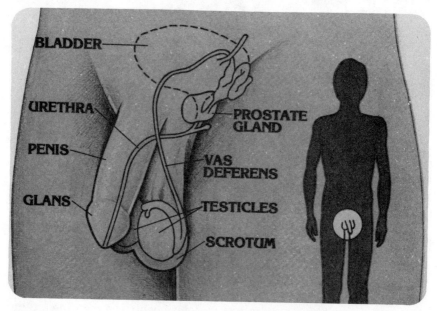

Penis: The male sex organ through which semen is discharged (ejaculation) during sexual intercourse. This organ is soft and spongy except when the male is sexually aroused (erection). Size and shape vary greatly, which does not affect ability to engage in intercourse.

Glans: The head of the penis and the most sexually sensitive part of a man's body because of its many nerve endings.

Foreskin (prepuce): A fold of skin covering the glans, but which may be pulled back from it. Removed during circumcision.

Testicles (testes): Two egg-shaped bodies which manufacture sperm and produce testosterone, the male sex hormone.

Scrotum: The pouch or sac of skin which houses the testicles. The outer location of the scrotum assures a slightly lower temperature. Normal body temperature of 98.6° would destroy the sperm.

Prostate: The gland which secretes a highly alkaline substance forming part of the seminal fluid and enabling sperm to move rapidly through the vagina.

Urethra: The tube through which urine is discharged from the body. In the male it also carries sperm during ejaculation.

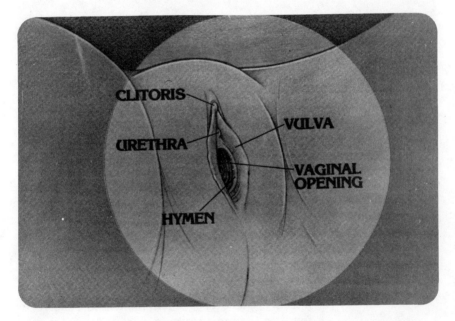

Vagina: The muscular tube running from the uterus to its external opening in the vulva. The vagina can stretch to accommodate any size penis during sexual intercourse. Also called the birth canal because the infant passes from the uterus through the vagina during delivery.

Vulva: The visible outward genital parts of a female.

21

Labia majora: The outward lips or folds of skin surrounding the vaginal opening.

Labia minora: The inner lips of the vaginal opening, located inside the labia majora.

Clitoris: Corresponds to the penis in the male, although much smaller. Contains an abundance of nerve endings, enabling it to be the most sexually excitable portion of the female body. When stimulated by friction, the clitoris enables a woman to reach orgasm. (However, because of abundant nerve endings in the vulval area, females can reach orgasm even when the clitoris has been surgically removed.)

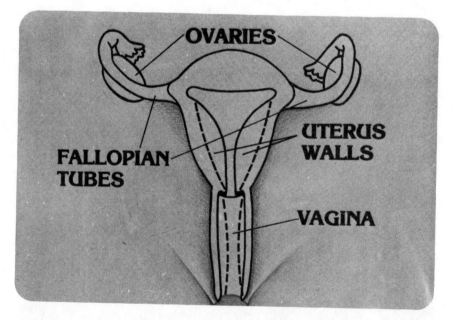

Ovary: The female organ which produces the ova (egg cells). Hormones secreted by the two ovaries prepare the uterus each month to receive a fertilized ovum. A single egg is normally discharged in each monthly female reproductive cycle through a process called ovulation.

Fallopian tubes: Two tubes leading from the ovaries to the uterus. Fertilization of egg by the sperm usually occurs here (conception). Then the fertilized egg travels to the uterus, where it is implanted and begins to grow and develop into a child (pregnancy).

Uterus (womb):	The small, muscular female organ shaped like an upside-down pear, in which the fetus (infant) develops. The uterus has the capacity to stretch to accommodate the growing child (children) and then return to almost normal size after delivery.

Being familiar with our bodies is important, of course. But emotional factors affect a couple's sexual relationship too. In fact, most sexual "problems" originate in our thoughts and feelings.

LOVING FEELINGS ARE IMPORTANT—ALL DAY LONG

Although many people assume sexual intercourse begins with the act, preparation ideally occurs all day long. Some husbands and wives consider morning the best time of day for intercourse. Other couples regard the first moments of the day as a special, private time before the demands of their daily lives take over.

"I've always hated getting up in the morning!" says Phyllis, "but now Paul and I set the alarm 15 minutes early every day and neither of us would miss that quiet time. Just beginning the day by hearing I'm precious to Paul, that I'm desirable ... to lie close in bed and hold each other ... well, it starts the day off right. We pray together, too, and that reminds us that God is in charge of our lives, guarding and guiding us. Those few minutes give me a peace and a joy about our life together. All day I remember being held and loved, and I can't wait to get the kids to bed so Paul and I can be alone again!"

During the day expressions of love—a pat in a strategic spot, an embrace, a look, a private joke—all set the stage for lovemaking. (By the way, parents shouldn't be self-conscious about embracing in front of their children. Such displays of affection speak volumes about what marriage can be, and will accomplish far more than any "sex talks" or books we may give them.)

"When Paul and I do have some time alone, we can give each other all our attention," continues Phyllis. "Our sexual relationship is good, but it's constantly changing. Sometimes we both want intercourse; other times one of us is really feeling sexy but the other can take it or leave it. If we've been feeling distant, we may decide that making love might be just the thing to make us feel close again. If we're feeling down and discouraged, one or both of us may need sex to reassure us. And, of course, if one or the other has had a rough day we might be just plain exhausted—too beat to want anything but sleep when we hit that bed!"

The experience of Paul and Phyllis shows that the quality of our sexual relationship varies with our moods, our state of health, how tired we are, the closeness we feel—or even with something completely removed from the marriage, such as work tensions.

SHIFTING GEARS

So how do we shift gears and turn our thoughts from our daily problems to each other? There are many ways. Some like to take a shower together or to give each other a body massage. Some listen to music or read poetry, while others prefer to just lie close together waiting for desire to build. And still others go right into foreplay.

Foreplay simply means "what comes before." This can include anything a couple finds mutually pleasing. In general terms it describes the caressing of each other's erogenous zones—commonly the nipple areas (both sexes), buttocks, the penis, and the clitoris. Indeed, these areas have a high concentration of nerve endings, making them the most sexually excitable parts of the body.

But once again thoughts and feelings are the key. If a couple is feeling close, loving, and desirous of each other, a touch—anywhere— is sexually exciting. But if there is fear or pain, disapproval, rejection or guilt, arousal may be extremely slow or nonexistent.

Many couples are unaware that allowing ample time beforehand is often the key to mutually satisfying sexual intercourse.

A wife may be slower to become fully aroused, while her husband may be more quickly excited. If the couple immediately engages in intercourse, it's quite likely the husband will ejaculate quickly, causing the penis to return to its normal state—soft and spongy. The wife, however, may just be getting aroused and is thus left unsatisfied.

In all too many marriages a pattern is established that almost guarantees a couple will have problems. "We go to bed and Ron announces it's time for sex," says Cathy. "He may take a minute or two to stimulate me manually, but then he doesn't want to wait anymore. In no time he has ejaculated and is ready for sleep. Then I lie there wondering whether I'm frigid."

SEXUAL DIFFICULTIES

Women who do not reach orgasm for one reason or another are often labeled "frigid," either by themselves or by their partners. The term has commonly been understood to mean a complete lack of sexual response, which is rarely true. Today the term "orgasmic impairment" is more often used. The causes vary, but like Cathy many women simply need more stimulation in order to reach orgasm.

Nor are women "born frigid," as is often supposed. Instead they are conditioned by factors in their upbringing or by some traumatic experiences. Those with deep-seated emotional problems may need counseling.

It also happens occasionally that a wife experiences unexpected difficulty in reaching her usual orgasm. Causes differ widely—underlying health problems, fatigue, emotional problems, or sustained concern over family problems. There's no need to panic. Almost certainly such occasions are individual incidents of no great significance. Extra love and reassurance can be helpful.

A woman who is aroused but doesn't reach orgasm may experience a feeling of heaviness in the pelvic area, caused by enlargement of blood vessels. Women who have had children may find this uncomfortable because pregnancy and giving birth permanently increase the blood supply to the vulva. This discomfort is relieved when a woman reaches orgasm, along with the release of sexual tensions.

Of course, there are male sexual difficulties, too. For instance, some men ejaculate almost instantly upon entry. Others do so long before their wives reach orgasm. This problem is called "premature ejaculation." Some contributing factors may be previous masturbation or illicit sex experiences which can condition the male to quick ejaculation. Or the husband may have the opposite problem and be extremely slow to reach ejaculation and climax. Some men may experience difficulty in obtaining—or maintaining—an erection. This is most often a problem with the older male.

Any problem in the area of sexual intercourse is now commonly called "sexual dysfunction," meaning that what should be normal and natural as ordained by God has become a troubled area. The cause is rarely physical. It's worth emphasizing that in most cases this is merely a sign that there's a problem—somewhere. Very often the couple's total relationship is less than thriving and their sexual difficulties only reflect that condition.

On the other hand, a couple's sexual difficulties can carry over into other areas of their marriage. "A couple of years ago I was really depressed, and our sexual relationship suffered," related Les. "I felt little interest in having sex with Evie, and every time we tried I was really slow. Sometimes I couldn't get an erection at all. Other times it wouldn't last. It was miserable, and I felt like a complete dud!

"After awhile I just avoided sex—even took to 'falling asleep' on the family room couch, just so I wouldn't have to admit I was afraid to try. I kept my distance and told myself Evie must be turning to someone else. Why not? I sure wasn't much good!

"Finally one day she sat me down and said she'd been to see a counselor," continued Les. "She made me promise to go too, and I finally did, dragging my feet all the way. He made me see that my problem was worry over business. Evie was just great the whole time—never let me forget that she loved me, no matter what. Now our sex life is better than ever. I guess that trouble was probably a blessing in disguise."

Unfortunately, many spouses react to sexual difficulties as Les did at first—by viewing themselves as faulty or second-rate. They prefer avoidance of sexual intercourse to possible "failure." Their distancing causes them to be even less sure of themselves, and it becomes a vicious circle. But a warm, loving, determined spouse can usually turn the situation around, as Evie did.

SOME "PROBLEMS" ARE NOT REALLY PROBLEMS

Many couples needlessly try for perfectly synchronized orgasms. While pacing oneself with one's partner is desirable, it's not really important whether both have an orgasm simultaneously. The only requirement is that both feel emotionally satisfied.

For even if pacing is perfect and both husband and wife reach climax together, the quality of orgasm is seldom of the same intensity from one occasion to the next. On occasion one may feel, to use a cliché, that there are skyrockets; another time one may experience just a warm, pleasant feeling. Such variations are normal.

Some books, magazines, novels, movies, television, and even locker room talk might try to give the impression that couples have marathon sex each night of the week. Thus we may feel we're not living up to some elusive performance standard, that perhaps we're undersexed. We might also think, after being exposed to the media, that if we only have intercourse in "the same old way" there must be something wrong with us.

The *only* criterion worth bothering about is whether each spouse is satisfied with their relationship. There are great variations in sex drives and the frequency of intercourse. There are solid marriages where one partner or the other seldom or never reaches orgasm but is completely content. But if *both* partners are satisfied with their sexual relationship it is "right" for them.

THE IMPORTANCE OF WORDS

"Ralph and I don't talk much about sex," says Pat. "At times our lovemaking just seems mechanical. I think he should sense what pleases me. I shouldn't have to tell him!"

Like Pat and Ralph, many couples hesitate to tell each other what they enjoy. For instance, a wife may wish her husband took more time during foreplay so that she would be more fully aroused. Or either spouse may want to be touched in a different manner or in another spot but doesn't say anything because it might be taken as criticism.

Learning to communicate our desires positively without shame or embarrassment is essential.

One can also communicate by touch or by a sign. The question is: Does my partner know what pleases me? Do I know what pleases my partner?

THE FREEDOM OF MARRIAGE

Another essential ingredient of a satisfactory sexual relationship is complete freedom with each other—the freedom to lose oneself, to forget about such useless questions as:

Does he (she) think I'm too fat? too flat?

Undersized?

What does he (she) think of me as a sexual partner?

Am I doing this right?

What will she (he) think if . . .?

Will this time be as good as last time? better?

Within the lifelong marriage commitment we can find such freedom. And love is the security factor, the freedom-giver. Feeling secure with each other enables each of us simply to enjoy each other.

REVERENCING CHRIST IN OUR MARRIAGE

In Christ neither the husband nor wife needs to dominate the other. In the Christian marriage we:

Submit to one another out of reverence for Christ.

Ephesians 5:21 NIV

Those words mean we're to put the other first—before our own needs and wants—because of our common love for Christ.

If we see our lives in that context, we need have no anxiety about old roles or new roles. And we're careful not to knowingly say or do things that would hurt our marriage partner.

"I used to embarrass Michelle in front of others," said Stan. "Oh, I always got a laugh! But I never noticed her reaction. Then when she was cool to me I'd say, 'What's wrong with you, anyway?' Took me awhile to figure it out. In fact, Michelle let me have it one day after our guests left. Once I saw what it meant to her—how it really hurt her—I quit."

"When we had that memorable fight, Stan let me know he didn't appreciate *my* attitude, either," said Michelle, smiling. "I was fond of letting him know I didn't need him or anybody else. I guess I was getting even with him. But when I thought about it I realized I wouldn't appreciate that from Stan, either. We both learned something!"

The truth is that both husband and wife need each other's love and emotional support. Most of us need—and want—a sexual relationship as well. Within marriage there are no unspeakable subjects, no rules except the law of love—concern for each other as persons, genuine caring for each other, valuing of each other as masterpieces of God's creation.

And that's true whether 22, lean and shapely, or 72 and full of bulges and wrinkles!

THE IMPORTANCE OF LOVING—BEFORE, DURING, AND AFTER

God lifted us above the animals by giving us the ability to love. That love assures that our attraction is not based on appearance and/or performance. That love ensures that even after intercourse husband and wife will want to show their continuing love for each other.

Carol says, "I love Reed dearly—always have—and I know he loves me. That didn't keep us from having our problems, though. Reed used to roll over and just go to sleep right after intercourse. I tried to make him understand how much it would mean to have him hold me then, but my words never made a dent.

"After awhile I began to resent it," continues Carol. "I felt used, as if I were some kind of sexual convenience, to be enjoyed and then ignored. Finally, when our sex lives had gone from pretty good to terrible, Reed began to get worried. That time when I told him how I felt he was ready to listen—and understand.

"Now we hold each other close after we have intercourse. It's a special time for me—and for Reed. In fact, Reed shows affection a lot more than he used to. I suppose it sounds silly, but I want to be loved as a person, all the time, not just when my husband wants sex!"

So a word to the wise: Partners need reassurance they're loved 24 hours a day, seven days a week, if there's to be continuing, lifelong desire. For most couples that kind of atmosphere guarantees a good relationship in all areas, including sex.

DON'T OVERLOOK THE OBVIOUS

All this presupposes, of course, that husbands and wives are considerate of each other in their bodily habits. Perfume and after-shave lotion are dispensable, but cleanliness and pleasant body smells are not. Frequent showers or baths, freshly brushed teeth, the use of deodorants, all make us nicer to be near.

It may be well to mention that the uncircumcised male should be especially careful to cleanse under the foreskin. A substance called smegma accumulates there and gives off an unpleasant odor if not washed away regularly. Smegma can also collect around the female clitoris.

As for the female who wonders whether she needs to douche to prevent vaginal odor, most gynecologists agree that the vagina is designed by God to be self-cleaning. Therefore douches are unnecessary, although most are harmless. Simple cleanliness of the vaginal area is sufficient. (However, should a woman notice a profuse, foul-smelling discharge, she should consult her doctor as she may have a vaginal infection—which is *not* the same as venereal disease.) Incidentally, the douche is totally useless as a birth control measure.

Fear of pregnancy can inhibit a couple's sexual relationship, although modern methods of birth control have largely eliminated that prospect. Whichever method a couple chooses to use, it's important to follow directions carefully and to bear in mind that *no* method—except abstinence—is 100% dependable.

Another requisite often overlooked is the importance of good physical condition. Just as optimum health and adequate rest enable us to perform our daily work more satisfactorily, so they also help in the sexual area. In fact, just going to bed earlier can rejuvenate a lagging sex life between two chronically underrested partners.

It bears mentioning, too, that alcohol, drugs (including some prescribed medications), anxiety, poor diet, depression, or lack of exercise can be detrimental. Any of them can lessen or even destroy sexual desire.

Health impairments or handicaps can be disadvantages, certainly, but they don't interfere with sexual function as much as many people imagine. (Check with your doctor if in doubt.) In general, as with so many other things, our ability to continue sexual activity depends mostly on our attitude and our thinking.

At any stage of life, if there are serious problems which don't seem to respond to our own efforts, it's often helpful to consult a counselor. Our pastor or doctor may be able to give good advice or to recommend someone they know to be reliable. And they'll understand should we not feel comfortable talking with them.

For the Christian couple, however, there is one Counselor to consult before all others. Unfortunately we often think of our sexual nature as being something we would never mention to God. Yet *He* created us as we are—sexual beings; *He* implanted in us the desire for our marriage partner; *He* made sexual intercourse possible.

Doesn't it seem logical He would hear our prayers concerning our own sexual lives?

QUESTIONS FROM COUPLES

Differences in Sex Drive

We have a good marriage in most ways, but we're on totally different wave-lengths when it comes to how often we have sex. Any suggestions?

Answer: Differences in sex drive are common because we're all individuals. Usually a lower-intensity sex drive stems from attitudes acquired during childhood or as a result of past experiences. If these differences are causing severe problems, professional counseling is advisable.

For most couples, however, the first step is understanding and admitting their problem is *mutual*, recognizing that neither is "right" or "wrong." Next comes talking with each other, honestly and with consideration. Usually such discussion will considerably ease tensions, and the partners can then arrive at a compromise that will meet the needs of both.

Sex Therapy

My husband and I are having problems with our sex life. We've worked with a marriage counselor, but it hasn't helped. How do we find one of those sex therapists we keep hearing about?

Answer: Talk to your pastor or physician and ask for a recommendation. Lacking that, call your county mental health center or your local medical society. Some colleges, also, have research facilities or can direct you to a qualified therapist.

Once you begin counseling, don't feel you must stay if the therapist says or does things that you think are wrong. Continually ask the Lord's guidance and then trust your instincts.

Both you and your husband must have a good rapport with the therapist—must feel at ease and find it easy to communicate freely—or nothing will be accomplished.

Disability and Sexual Ability

Can a person who is paralyzed have sexual intercourse?

Answer: Each case is individual, differing with the cause of the disability. For instance, in the case of injury to the spine it depends on the nature and location of the damage. Some disabled men are capable of erection and ejaculation; others are not. If ejaculation can occur, the sperm is usually fertile.

For those men not able to obtain an erection there are prosthetic devices available, some of them surgically implanted, which make intercourse possible. Typically the victim of a spinal injury will not experience the usual physical sensations. However, he usually derives great emotional satisfaction from meeting his partner's sexual needs. It's possible for a couple to enjoy a warm, close sexual relationship even though they cannot engage in the usual intercourse.

The situation is less complex for the female who is partially or totally immobile, if only because a female does not require an erection to be a sexual partner.

Male Impotence

What causes male impotence? Is there any treatment?

Answer: First, be aware that the term "impotent" describes the male who is consistently unable to achieve and/or maintain an erection. That's very different from what's involved in aging, which may mean that it takes a man longer to achieve an erection. (For some it may take up to 15 minutes.)

Causes for impotency cover a wide range—*emotional* (stress, worries), *physical* (diabetes mellitus, hormonal imbalance, liver/kidney failure, etc.) or *prescription-drug related* (antianxiety drugs, antidepressant medications, tranquilizers, etc.). Often the same relief of medical symptoms can be obtained by changing the medication—or even the brand of the drug. Such a simple change has eliminated problems of impotency and/or loss of sexual drive within a short time.

Consult a urologist or other medical professional to determine possible physical or emotional causes for impotency.

As a last resort, thousands of men have had a penile implant surgically placed to restore sexual function. There are at least two types, both undetectable when the recipient is clothed and sometimes even when nude. Studies show that most couples are happy with the results.

Explaining Parents' Forced Marriage to Child

Our eldest child was born after we'd been married only six months. When we talk about avoiding premarital sex, our child, now a teenager, taunts us with reminders such as, "You're not so perfect yourselves!" How do we handle this?

Answer: Perhaps you can share some of the pain that accompanied that situation. For instance, most couples believe their life together would have been happier if they'd had time to adjust to marriage and to each other before the birth of their child. Think back. What was it like? Were there feelings of hurt and resentment? of shame? of regret?

Obviously your child already knows the facts. Now share the emotions you experienced at that time. It's also crucial that your child is convinced of being wanted—if not when conceived, at least at birth. Emphasize that you loved each other and your coming child—enough to establish a home, to battle the odds and make your marriage work. Be honest about your struggles, but also talk of how precious your child is to you.

Share your feelings of guilt, repentance, and forgiveness; what you have gone through and how you feel the love of Christ. Ask for forgiveness from your child, too.

4. The Single Parent Views Sexuality: Gift or Burden?

I have the strength to face all conditions by the power that Christ gives me.

Philippians 4:13 TEV

The number of single parents is growing at a rapid rate. There are the widowed, the divorced, and those who are neither but are raising one or more children. The burden of being mother *and* father can be staggering. There is often no shoulder to cry on, no one to offer words of support.

Nor is one's sexual nature frozen. Needs continue, not only for relief of sexual tensions but even more for the affirmation that we are loved, desired, valued—as persons, not just parents.

Whether or not one yearns for a mate, the key to surviving single parenthood lies in accepting our situation and relying on Christ's strength, not our own. Indeed, it's as true for the single parent as for those who are wed: God is in charge of our lives, and no experience—good or bad—is wasted with our gracious God.

Yet the single parent has uncertainties peculiar to singlehood. Can a mother be a good role model for a son? Can a father wisely guide a daughter? Is it possible to be all things to all people?

Probably not. Fortunately, most single parents are aware that their children need a balanced viewpoint, and they try to ensure ample contact with people of the same sex as the missing parent. It helps the child to identify, to learn, to model in a way that's not quite possible with just one parent.

FINDING SUBSTITUTES

"I could see that my daughter needed a woman as a friend—someone to confide in," said Marv, "but all our family was a thousand miles away and we hadn't lived in this area long enough to be well acquainted. Fortunately our church sponsors a group for Christian singles, and one evening I felt free enough to tell the others that my 13-year-old daughter, Kim, had me worried. I sensed she needed more than I could give her, so I asked whether anyone had any suggestions.

"One of the new gals spoke up and said she had a son about the same age who needed some help with sports and she felt just as inadequate as I. Soon the others were spilling their own worries, so we worked out an informal exchange program. Now several of us get together in each other's homes on weekends. Sometimes the gals all go shopping while we guys watch the football games. Then we share a pizza for supper. Most of us aren't thinking of marriage right now, so there's no pressure. But we all need friends—and this arrangement fills the bill for the kids as well as for us adults.

"Now that some time has passed, I can handle my loss," said Marv thoughtfully, "but at first the emptiness of my life—in spite of the kids—seemed almost more than I could manage. I guess I was going through that grief process they talk about. The only thing that has kept me going is the support of my friends in that group. They know firsthand where I am."

For some single parents, living in the present moment—without a partner, without a sexual relationship—is almost unthinkable. Some frequent the singles bars, some the dating bureaus, all looking for someone who cares.

"I couldn't handle being alone night after night," said Shari, "so I started hanging around at the local 'meat markets.' I found that most of the guys there wanted only one thing—a warm body. *Any* warm body! They told me just what I wanted to hear—that I'm attractive, that I'm sexy, that I turned them on. And it had been so long since anyone had said such things that it was music to my ears. But I soon realized they didn't want a relationship, only instant gratification. I guess since I was hanging around they had a right to expect that's what I wanted, too. It wasn't long, though, before I began to feel cheap and even more depressed.

"So I started going to the singles group at church. There I found some real friends—people who know my needs because they share them. They give me the encouragement that I hunger for, the sense of being a worthwhile person. I'm beginning to like myself again."

Shari exemplifies the longing many single parents have. Their need makes them extremely vulnerable and leads many into shallow relationships and "one-night stands" that afford no lasting fulfillment.

DEALING WITH SEXUAL TENSIONS

Yet single parents do retain their sexual natures. How does one deal with these needs and still live by Christian principles?

Psychologists say sexual expression is a primary human need, second only to food. Research also shows, however, that putting off one's sexual needs does not damage a person, either physically or emotionally. Nor does it eventually cause distorted personality traits. There are millions of single persons who are perfectly well-adjusted and fulfilled without having a sexual relationship.

Christian counselors would agree with those conclusions, but add another dimension. They point out that Christ's grace and strength are sufficient for all our needs and that one's sexual desires can be put aside for a time with no damage.

It's important to remember, too, that even though alone, we're still examples for our children. How we handle our sexual natures will be noted and mentally filed away. When 15-year-old Cara was growing up, she often found one of a succession of men sharing her divorced mother's bed and board. "It was always 'Uncle Jack' or 'Uncle Bill' or 'Uncle Pete,' but I knew what was going on. When I got to be about 11, I guess she decided I might catch on. Then Mom started giving me another line—said she was visiting her 'cousins' on weekends. Funny how interested she got in her 'family' all of a sudden!

"Last week Mom came home from work early and found me in bed with my boyfriend, and she hit the ceiling! Can you beat that? As far as I'm concerned she's got a nerve calling me names!"

Cara's mother, of course, handled her sexual needs in the wrong way—and so did Cara. Undoubtedly she was lonely and vulnerable and drifted into quick encounters. Such shallow relationships merely compound the problems a single parent already faces.

But each person must deal with his or her own sexual nature. A good general principle is to remain active—to become involved with church activities, sports, hobbies, community needs, etc. If the local Christian community has no singles group, perhaps all that's needed is one person to be a spark plug. Actually, anything that keeps one busy and gives a sense of purpose is worth pursuing. Breaking out of old habit patterns and accepting new challenges is an invigorating way to strengthen self-esteem, to meet new people and, incidentally, to sublimate sexual desires.

AVOIDING HARMFUL PATTERNS

One harmful pattern may occur when children spend time with their other parent. Either parent may "pump" the children for information about their former spouse. Whether the youngsters realize what's happening depends somewhat on their age. But it can be difficult for children, because it puts them squarely in the middle.

Nor is it good to try to buy children's affection and loyalty. "Sam and I both love our kids. That didn't stop just because we were divorced. But it suddenly became important to 'prove' we loved them," said Greta, smiling. "Naturally, it didn't take Sean and Elizabeth long to figure out they could play Dad against Mom and vice versa. For awhile there they had a good thing going—until Sam and I wised up. Fortunately we're on pretty good terms, so we talked about it and decided to cut out the stupidity.

"Now that Sam has remarried, I try, too, to help the kids adjust to having another woman in their dad's home. I figure no matter how *I* feel about his new wife, it will make it harder for them if I keep bad-mouthing her and their dad. So I try to be as positive as I can—about everything."

Greta's decision is wise. Too often past bitterness causes one parent to continually tear down the other. Yet children need to be able to identify with both parents, to trust both parents. Anything else may reinforce the child's sense of being rejected by the missing parent, a feeling that can be a very harmful force in the child's attitude—for life.

"After my dad walked out on us, my mom told me all about him," said 29-year-old Debbie. "I heard all the dirt, all the sleazy tricks he pulled on her—over and over and over. You bet your life I didn't want anything to do with him. Or any man! If that's what marriage means, forget it!"

Such alienation can only be destructive to all. Rather, we want to assure our children that we love them—hug them, give them a reassuring pat on the shoulder—to speak often of our affection for them, our pride in them. They need that love from us, and we need to show it.

WORKING OUT ANGER IS IMPORTANT

A common situation is that of hostility between the child and whichever parent he or she holds responsible for the breakup of the marriage (or sometimes even the death of the spouse). The lonely parent may find such consistent resentment shattering. It's important to help children work through such feelings. Otherwise their anger and guilt can gnaw at them for years and cause many other, more serious problems.

35

"It's been two years now since Milt and I were divorced, and Stacey hadn't been able to talk about it in all that time," said Alice. "I guess I just left her alone because I didn't know what to do. Besides, I had enough problems of my own! But she became a different girl . . . began doing so poorly in school and seemed so troubled that her teacher called me in for a conference.

"Turned out Mrs. Petersen is divorced too, and knew how it had affected her children. She asked whether Stacey ever talked about it, and I said, 'No, she tries to avoid the subject—can't seem to get the words out.' Mrs. Petersen recommended I get a book about divorce—one written for children—and give it to Stacey. I found several at the library and took one home. We read through it together. One of us would read a page or two and then I could ask, 'Have you ever felt that way?'

"At last it was out in the open," continued Alice, "and it was like breaking a logjam. Stacey spilled out all her feelings. It hurt, of course, to see it, but it helped me understand why she's been so withdrawn and sullen lately. Once she unloaded, we were able to talk. I could sense a change in her almost immediately. I think Stacey has finally started to resolve her feelings. Our communication is better now, and I believe the worst is over."

Hostility is only one of the stages youngsters may go through. Another may be guilt. "My folks split up when I was 11," said Claudia. "I remembered all the times when Mom said 'yes' and Dad said 'no.' They had terrible fights over me! So when Dad walked out, I just knew it was because of me. My guilt gnawed at me all my growing-up years. I saw myself as a terrible person—one who'd broken up her own parents' marriage. After all, no one ever told me otherwise. Dad was gone, and my mom became kind of withdrawn and distant. That only made me more certain I was to blame."

Claudia and Stacey illustrate a point worth noting: Children often have a more difficult time in dealing with their parents' divorce than adults imagine. So it's important to be understanding and supportive—to allow them to have their feelings. If they're to have the healthy self-image so necessary to be able to relate lovingly to others, such troubling emotions should be expected—respected—drawn out—talked out—resolved.

OTHER ASPECTS OF SINGLE PARENTHOOD

Being a single parent is never easy. However, there *are* positive aspects. For example, one is free to act without considering another's wishes or feelings. One can decide on the life-style one wants for the family and proceed without criticism or resistance from one's spouse.

Not to be overlooked, either, is the closeness that can develop between parent and child. "When Gail died I wanted to die, too," said

Will. "I didn't see how I could possibly keep the family together. Penny was an adolescent and Brent was just 10. How would I handle a teenage daughter?

"But I guess when you have to, somehow you manage. Trying to cope with the loss and the grief and get the place organized was awful for all of us. But little by little we got it all together.

"The pressures are still heavy," Will continued, "yet I've discovered there's been a bonus. I probably know my kids far better than I would have if Gail were alive, because I pretty much left the child-raising up to her. Now I'm the one that's directly involved. And I love it!

"I had to get in touch with my own feelings, too," said Will. "In the beginning I was up half the night—remembering, weeping, praying. I had to come to terms with my loss, I suppose. I still miss Gail terribly, but now I know we will survive—and probably be closer than we ever could have been otherwise."

ATTITUDES COUNT

Whether married or single, how we feel about our lives and ourselves depends on our values and attitudes. Our first priority is that of every Christian parent—to establish and maintain a right relationship with God, with ourselves, and with our children. For no human being can completely fill our need and give us deep, abiding joy—not our child, not our friend, not even a marriage partner.

As always, those elusive qualities known as happiness and contentment come only from our loving God—the Source of all that's good.

5. *Parenthood: The Changes Begin*

Children are a gift from the Lord; they are a real blessing.

Psalm 127:3 TEV

When a wife becomes pregnant, the couple enters a new stage in their relationship. They can no longer concentrate only on themselves—or on each other. And no matter how delighted they are, they're bound to wonder what changes this pregnancy will bring to their relationship.

Producing a child is a bit of an ego trip. Father feels important and protective. Every time he looks at his pregnant wife, he's reminded that his child is growing within her. A part of himself is being reproduced.

Mother feels very special, too, concentrating on eating the right foods, getting enough rest—taking good care of herself for her baby's sake. Even the discomforts and awkwardness of advancing pregnancy seem somehow noble. After all, she's nurturing a new human being, the evidence of the love she and her husband share.

Often a couple finds this a time when they draw closer than ever before. They share a mutual dream. And if at times their sexual relationship suffers, well, they assure each other they'll get back to normal after the baby is born. And at last that happy day arrives.

In a few days the three of you went home from the hospital. You were a family at last. And you soon discovered that nothing—*nothing*—was quite the same. Before too many days had passed you began to suspect that perhaps it never would be as it had been before. (And parents everywhere would tell you that you were absolutely correct!)

For one thing, a helpless newborn infant reigns supreme. When that tiny bit of humanity lets loose with one of its amazingly loud screams, everyone jumps to answer the summons. Thus many a young father, though he loves his child dearly, feels that his home—his castle—has been taken over by an intruder and no one has time for him.

The mother, on the other hand, is exhausted from middle-of-the-night feedings and the strain of wondering whether she's correctly handling all the new situations which confront her. Because of natural hormonal changes she may be feeling decidedly weepy, too, and it's not unusual for father to come home to a house where both mother and child are crying.

BABIES MAKE A DIFFERENCE—IN MANY AREAS

Even after a wife has her doctor's permission to resume sexual relations with her husband, she may not seem as interested as before, largely because she has more things on her mind at this stage and may still feel insecure as a mother. Then, too, she seems always to have one ear cocked for the baby's cry, which comes at the most inopportune times. The new father may wonder if she'll ever again give him her undivided attention.

"Ever since we had the baby, Jill thinks I can always wait—for everything," says Danny, "for meals, for conversation—even for lovemaking. I love that kid and I know Jill loves me, but I really begin to wonder who rates around here!"

Such feelings are normal, for both husband and wife. The wise husband tries to be patient, and the prudent wife does all she can to let her husband know he's still important. If the baby is fed and dry, she realizes an occasional bit of fussing won't damage the child for life, so she concentrates on her husband—her lover.

One of the major reasons for putting the baby to sleep somewhere other than in the parents' bedroom is because husband and wife need time alone, to focus on each other, to love and be loved as persons, not parents.

THE NO. 1 TASK OF PARENTS

The most important task that faces the new father and mother is *not* the obvious child care and support. Their major job, starting with

Day One, is to provide their child with constant, accepting love. As Christians we believe that kind of love has only one source: God.

> Dear friends, let us love one another, because love comes from God....
> We love because God first loved us.
>
> 1 John 4:7 & 19 TEV

No less vital is to have the same attitude toward each other. The best things parents can do for their children is to love each other, for when parents feel loved themselves, they have an abundance of love to give their offspring. Such an atmosphere ensures a happy home where children will grow up well-adjusted, with good self-images and the foundation they need for their own adult lives.

The child's sense of being accepted or rejected, his or her self-image and value system for the rest of life are greatly influenced during the first five years of life. Stay-at-home mothers may see those years as a period of confinement and hard work, with never a moment to call their own. (And in many ways that's true.) Yet all the time they're determining life values.

When both parents work away from home, it's of prime importance that there is as little turnover as possible in the person(s) providing child care, for a youngster needs stability. It's also vital that the person(s) who care for children have attitudes and values to which parents themselves subscribe. A child often spends more waking hours with a baby-sitter than with his parents, so that person's life-style and views inevitably carry great weight with the child. Is that reassuring? Or does it make us uneasy?

Reading this may fill many of us with remorse and guilt. If so, be assured: *All* parents make mistakes. *All* parents have times when they feel antagonism toward their child. *All* parents at times communicate attitudes they later regret. And few totally agree with their baby-sitter's attitudes, even when the child's own grandparents fill that role. So what's a parent to do?

"Shucks!" says Great Grandma. "There's only one thing parents can do—same as we did and our folks before us. That's just ask the good Lord for wisdom and count on Him to take everything in our children's lives—even our mistakes—and turn it to good. He did it in Bible times. He still can!"

OUR CHILDREN COPY US

Each of us is a model for our children,
day after day,
year after year,
whether we wish to be or not.

What do we want our children to become? What do we want them to remember? No matter what we answer, the truth is that our children's strengths and weaknesses, the values they will have, their sexual attitudes, are determined more by what they see in us than by any other single factor. The timeworn expressions we've all heard are true:

* More is caught than taught.
* What you are speaks so loud I can't hear what you say.

"The idea that my kids are always watching, that they'll copy my faults as well as my good points, was almost more than I could handle," said Peg. "I thought I had to be perfect—tried to be sure my kids would be perfect, too. Made us all miserable! Then one day I realized it's not just up to me—that I can trust God's promises. After all, He gave us these children—or I should say, He loaned them to us."

Peg makes an important point. Our children are only entrusted to our care. Although part of us, they don't belong to us in the sense of possessions. Nor are they extensions of us. They are individuals in their own right.

Incidentally, seeing children as extensions of ourselves may be a reason why childless husbands or wives sometimes find the idea of adoption unappealing. They may worry that they'd be assuming the unknown, possibly disturbing traits of the biological parents. Some think an adopted child would never give them the same satisfaction (translate: ego gratification) as a child who displayed their own characteristics.

"A CHIP OFF THE OLD BLOCK"?

But any seasoned parent could set them straight in a few minutes, for it doesn't take long to learn that every child is an individual, full of surprises. Oh yes, that child bears genes and chromosomes from both sets of forebears. But which ones? Some character traits and body resemblances may be easily identifiable. However, it's not at all unusual for a child to look like a faded brown baby picture of a great-great-grandparent rather than resemble either parent.

Nor is it uncommon for a child to be, for instance, extremely strong-willed, although the offspring of mild-mannered parents. The mystery may be solved when Great-Aunt Harriet comes to visit, laughs and says, "Why, I'm not surprised. I remember my dad saying his father was the stubbornest man in six counties. Little Matthew is just a chip off his great-great-great grandad!"

The truth is there are no guarantees what a child will turn out to be. Nor are they lumps of clay that we can mold into the kind of person we'd like them to become. They are themselves. To be sure, some children are more easily guided, but that's about the most definite statement one can make. Our task is to help our children become the best *they* can be, as we point them to Christ, THE model for all Christians.

CHILDREN ARE SEXUAL BEINGS, TOO

It may be surprising to realize that our children are sexual beings from birth. For instance, a parent changing a male infant's diaper may accidentally stimulate the child and be shocked to realize the child is having an erection. Similarly, researchers tell us that baby girls have vaginal lubrication regularly. In fact, a little girl being bounced on her parent's knee may feel pleasant sensations and begin to make natural pelvic thrust movements.

This is *not* to say we should be afraid to touch our children or bounce them on our knees! It's merely to point out that all of us are born as sexual beings. Yet somehow the thought of a child's sexual nature is vaguely disturbing to many adults. We've all known, of course, that children ask questions about where babies come from, etc., but we've assumed this is simple curiosity. We may answer in great detail yet feel uncomfortable talking of such things with our youngsters. Children are naturally curious, true, but their sexual nature plays a part in such questioning too. It bears repeating: We are created by God to be sexual beings, from the very first day of our lives.

THOSE IMPORTANT FIRST TWO YEARS

During the first two years of life children get their foundation—establishment of their own gender and that of others, plus role behavior; a sense of body and self-image, along with motor co-ordination; a feeling of closeness (or estrangement) with other humans, especially parents; a realization they are welcomed into the family and accepted by those around. We build a sound, healthy base for the child by ample touching and closeness. When we care for the child, such as when changing diapers, we avoid facial expressions or remarks that hint any part or function of the body is distasteful to us or "dirty." This is "sex education" in its earliest form.

The same principle applies when children this age explore and may absent-mindedly or consciously touch their genitals.

During this stage of life as with all others, the most important influence is how the parents relate to each other, how they view their own sexuality. Far from being oblivious, the young child is constantly watching, evaluating, assimilating.

QUESTIONS NEW PARENTS WONDER ABOUT

Intercourse During Pregnancy

Is it okay to have intercourse during pregnancy?

Answer: Yes, almost always. Most obstetricians encourage couples to continue to have sexual intercourse, recognizing that husbands and their pregnant wives need this expression of love and closeness—perhaps more than ever.

However, as the wife's abdomen enlarges, a couple may find their usual position(s) uncomfortable and may wish to try other positions. If there are questions or if problems arise, ask your own physician. Most obstetricians advise pregnant females to avoid sexual intercourse during the final six weeks. (Many doctors counsel couples to deal with sexual tensions by mutual manual stimulation.)

Pregnant Wife Not Interested

My wife is eight months pregnant and doesn't seem much interested in lovemaking anymore. I know she loves me—but what's going on, anyway?

Answer: Studies show that almost all women lose much of their sexual desire during the latter three months of pregnancy. Also, they may reach orgasm less often, and when they do, the orgasm is less intense. It may be partly due to a woman's larger abdominal size, which makes sexual intercourse less comfortable. And since many women feel awkward, clumsy, and somewhat unattractive in the latter months of pregnancy, these emotions may play a large part, as well.

Probably the most helpful thing a loving husband can do is to give his wife lots of reassurance that he loves her, that she's still attractive to him, and that he knows they can successfully weather this period of their marriage.

Breastfeeding and Pregnancy

As long as I'm nursing my baby I can't become pregnant. Right?

Answer: Not necessarily. Although you may not have a menstrual period during that time, it's possible you may ovulate. Therefore you could become pregnant.

Childbirth's Effect on Vagina

Having a baby must stretch the vagina a lot. How does that affect sexual intercourse later?

Answer: A woman's vagina must stretch enough to accommodate the baby's head. It does go back to size, but like a rubber band that has been stretched it will be somewhat larger than before. With each birth there is more relaxation of the muscles. The vagina also loses some muscle tone as a woman gets older.

This may or may not make a difference in either partner's satisfaction. Many doctors recommend a simple exercise that can strengthen and tighten vaginal muscles. A woman is advised to contract the same muscles she would if she wished to stop the flow of urine, alternately contracting and relaxing these muscles about 20 times. Repeating the series 10 times daily will considerably tighten the vagina in three to four weeks. (In extreme cases of severe muscle damage, corrective surgery may be of help.)

6. The Preschool Years: Laying the Groundwork

Teach a child how he should live, and he will remember it all his life.
Proverbs 22:6 TEV

From ages three to six the child's picture of what it means to be male or female is strengthened. This forms a basic sense of appropriate behavior and begins to be part of the child's approach to life.

"Kevin and I used to think it was cute when our little girl and boy played house," said Belinda, "but when we really began to listen, it wasn't funny! 'Daddy' spent all his time in front of the TV, telling the 'children' to be quiet. 'Mommy' did nothing but complain about how tough her life was—how no one cared how hard she worked.

"One day we asked Aaron what a man does. He said, 'Well, he's gone a lot. When he comes home, everybody has to be quiet so he can rest. Daddies don't have to do anything at home.' Then we asked Alissa what a woman does, and she said, 'A woman does all the work, and nobody ever helps her unless she hollers. She never has time to play games or go to the park. And she looks mad all the time.'

"Once we realized what our children were learning from watching us, we decided to make some changes," continued Belinda. "Neither Kevin nor I liked the picture they were giving us. But it was simply a reflection of what our kids saw and heard."

As Belinda and Kevin found out, children learn their roles—what it means to be a male or a female—by watching us, and then they pattern (model) themselves after us. This is especially true during this age period, when children have fewer outside distractions. In fact, the parents' example is the central factor in the child's *self-identity development* from the very beginning and is imbedded for life.

On the other hand, although the child identifies mostly with the parent of the same sex, the other parent has an important influence too. For instance, a girl gets her idea of what a male should be largely from her father—or from another adult male who plays a major part in her life (an uncle, a grandfather, etc.). She also receives reinforcement of her own feminine nature. The same kind of thing occurs with boys and their mothers.

But children learn more than just role behavior from their parents. They either learn a loving God has a part in their daily life—or they don't. They also adopt emotional qualities such as a caring attitude or one that implies, "Don't bother me"; concern for others or insensitivity; love or coldness; kindness or belligerence; generosity or selfishness; patience or impatience.

Individual differences do count, but so does environment. For instance, a family's gloomy temperament may not be so much a hereditary trait as a behavior pattern acquired during the parents' childhood and passed on to the next generation.

OUTSIDE INFLUENCES

If our child attends a day-care center, a nursery school, or a preschool, it's vital that we evaluate especially the school's teachers and helpers, to determine their values and goals. We'll want to observe how staff members relate to the children—and each other. We'll look—and listen—to discover whether personnel and other children display the behavior and healthy attitudes we desire in our own child.

Although this may seem a time-consuming effort, it's not a waste. One of the young child's basic needs is constancy in child care. The youngster's stability is reinforced by long-term, secure relationships. That makes it advisable to do as much advance evaluation as possible, in order to avoid relocating the child frequently.

PRESCHOOLERS ARE CURIOUS ABOUT SEX

When the three- to six-year-old asks questions about sex, answer calmly, in the same manner and tone of voice as with any other subject. Give basic information, using correct terminology. Too often parents feel uneasy using terms such as uterus, vagina, and penis. So they may say something like, "The baby is growing in Mommy's tummy" or speak vaguely of "a seed from the father being planted" in the mother.

46

As a result the child may have troubling mental pictures of the baby growing in Mommy's tummy, alongside a cheeseburger and french fries. Or memories of digging and helping to plant seeds in the garden may cause a child to wonder how that has any connection with Mommy and Daddy. Therefore it's important to emphasize that the uterus, which is *near* the stomach, and the vagina are special places in a woman's body, made by God for a unique purpose.

No need to get clinical, though. Remember the mother in the old joke? When her three-year-old asked, "Where did I come from?" she immediately launched into a detailed explanation of conception and birth. When she paused at last and asked if he had any questions the little boy said, "Yeah. But what was the name of that town where we lived before?"

In other words, answer the questions that are *asked*. Children will absorb only what they are ready to understand, so no great harm will be done if we overexplain. Sharing a book with you child can be helpful, too. Book One of the Learning about Sex series is written just for this age group. In *Why Boy and Girls Are Different* author Carol Greene delightfully captures a child's sense of wonder about sexuality, God's creation, and the warmth of family life.

QUESTIONS FROM PARENTS

Child Sleeping with Parents

Our three-year-old has developed a habit of coming into our bedroom in the middle of the night and crawling into our bed. Is this harmful?

Answer: Taking a fearful child into your bed on occasion will not cause problems, but don't let it become a habit. The child may experience some feelings of sexual arousal which are confusing, perhaps even frightening, upon sleeping with the parent(s)—feelings which could cause later problems. (This is true even though you are careful to avoid any possibility of direct sexual stimulation such as rubbing against you, etc., and would immediately put an end to it should the child make any moves in that direction.)

Be aware, also, that a child may deliberately try to come between you and your spouse, both literally and figuratively. The child may appear delighted to plop down between Mommy and Daddy, but such action may involve competitive feelings with the parent of the same sex. (Such feelings are common at this age.)

Child Interrupting Parents' Intercourse

Our child walked into our bedroom while we were having intercourse. How should we have handled it?

Answer: Young children—even infants—can be upset by seeing or hearing their parents engaging in sexual intercourse. The child may confuse the movements, the sounds, and facial expressions as violence similar to wrestling, fighting, or in some way hurting each other.

If your child walks into your bedroom unannounced, in the midst of intercourse, ask him or her to leave, firmly, so he knows that you're to have privacy in your own bedroom. Or try to conquer your embarrassment and make a brief explanation—perhaps something like this:

"Daddy and I love each other very much, you know that. And sometimes when we're together we want to hold each other very, very close—to touch each other all over and almost be a part of each other's body. That's the way God made married people. It's one way we show how much we love each other.

"We love you, too, but we want to be alone now, so please go back to bed. And from now on please remember to knock on our door and wait for us to answer before you come into our room, because this is our private territory."

Establish a family policy early. Impress upon them that courteous people always knock when doors are closed—and that includes parents as well as children.

Locking the door is a simple solution, of course. However, children may become unduly curious and even build up disturbing ideas if the door is locked only at certain times. It's better to emphasize that your room is off-limits unless the door is open.

Nudity in the Home

Is it harmful for children to see their parents and/or siblings nude?

48

Answer: There is no right or wrong for the young child. If the parents are comfortable with their own standards, the children will be too. If children are accustomed from birth to seeing their parents nude, there will likely be no effect at all. Of course, children may have questions about their parents' bodies; for instance, a boy may want to know why his father's penis is larger or a girl may wonder why she doesn't have breasts like her mommy. Parents should answer such questions casually, reassuring the children they will also develop as maturity approaches.

Most siblings are quite unaware of each other's nudity in the early years. They usually accept each other's anatomical differences with little note once they've had their initial questions answered.

Of course, as children get older, they should be brought to realize that modesty requires some restrictions on nudity, even in the seclusion of the home.

7. Six to Nine: Branching Out

Jesus said, "Let the children come to Me and do not stop them, because the Kingdom of heaven belongs to such as these."

Matthew 19:14 TEV

At this stage of growing up the toddler phase is but a memory. The time when we hovered and could easily distract a misbehaving child is long gone, and the rebelliousness of adolescence has not yet begun. Therefore it's especially important that we communicate our values and why we hold them, including our faith in God. That means talking about how our faith relates to our family life and to our way of living. If we haven't done so before, we'll see they have an opportunity to attend Sunday school and we'll do everything we can to help them lay the foundation for a faith that lasts a lifetime.

And time grows short! Once children start attending school, the circle of people influencing them widens considerably. "Teacher" may become the supreme authority on everything. Children also develop close friendships with peers, who exert a powerful influence. Their perception of how to behave as male or female may change as they have more contact with families having differing life-styles.

Because children of this age group are not yet involved in dating, not yet experiencing personal sexual attraction, they'll accept our explanations and values more readily than in the future. For that reason it's a prime time to develop healthy, relaxed attitudes toward sex.

Parents should answer questions about sex calmly and frankly, but also look for opportunities to offer such information when the child has *not* asked. Open communication is not the total answer, however. Most attitudes that children adopt come more as a result of copying someone they admire. Especially their parents.

"The child guidance class I took was a big help to me," says Gwen. "It made me realize that no matter how crazy the world seems sometimes, no matter how many factors affect our children, Mark and I are the most important, most lasting influence of all. Our kids get most of their ideas of how to be a man or woman—a husband or wife—from watching us.

"My friend, Dina, who's a widow, was quite disturbed. After all, she's raising her children alone," continues Gwen. "But the teacher made us see that other people who are part of the wider family circle— like Dina's dad and her brother and the next-door neighbor—can also be good male role models. Understanding that helped ease her mind. Sure made us realize, though, how important it is to be careful about the people spending time with our children. They may be personal friends, but if we wouldn't want our kids to copy them, we'd better arrange to see those people at other times."

A TIME OF CURIOSITY

Children this age are curious—about everything. So you may find them "playing doctor" one day, giving you a natural opportunity to offer sex information. If you discover such play, be casual about it and avoid imparting—or implying—guilt or shame.

You might want to say something like, "Well, Joshua, I suppose you and Beth wanted to see if little girls and little boys are alike. Now you know that boys and girls are different. God made all boys the same and all girls the same."

This would be a good time to offer a positive substitute activity. You might want to say something like, "How would you two like a glass of milk? Want to come out in the kitchen and help me get things ready for lunch?"

TALKING ABOUT SEX

You may not want to talk in more detail unless both children are your own. If so, this would be an excellent time to go into more detail, correctly naming parts of the body. (Otherwise speak to your own child when you're alone.)

51

You may wish to say something like this: "God gives all boys special body parts that make them boys. One part is called a penis. When you urinate, Joshua, you use your penis. The water, which we call urine, comes out through a tube called the urethra, which is inside your penis. The tube is something like a soda straw. Girls have a urethra tube, too, but it's up inside their bodies, and the urine comes out through a little opening.

"Boys also have two testicles. They're shaped a bit like eggs. The testicles are enclosed in a sac of skin called the scrotum, and they're just behind the penis. Your body is getting ready now for when you grow up, Joshua, when you may want to be a daddy. The seed for making babies, which is called sperm, will come from the testicles and out the penis.

"You probably noticed that Beth is different. That's because God gives girls special body parts, too, but *inside* their bodies where you can't see them. Beth has a special place called a vagina and another special place called a uterus, just like every other girl.

"One of the things a girl can do when she grows up is to be a mommy. And the baby grows inside the mother's uterus, safe and warm, until it's big enough and strong enough to come out through the vagina and live on its own. That's the way you got here, you know. You grew in Mommy's uterus, and when you were all ready, you were born. And everybody loved you so much and was so happy to see you!"

Such an explanation will help to reinforce the child's self-identity as male or female—and also the feeling of being a loved, wanted part of the family. If it seems unnecessarily detailed, remember that it's wise to use correct terminology, remembering again that at any age children filter out what's beyond their understanding. On the other hand, if your child asks for more information, such as sexual intercourse, feel free to enlarge upon this explanation.

This can also be a good time to share a children's book with your son or daughter. The excellent books in this series are written from a Christian perspective. Book Two, *Where Do Babies Come From?* by Ruth Hummel, is written for children in grades one and two. For children in grades three through five, Book Three, *How You Are Changing*, by Jane Graver, would be just right. Read these books *with* your child. Be sensitive and ready to answer questions your child may be too timid to ask. Make it a special time of sharing and closeness. Once you're sure the child understands the content, you may wish to let your youngster keep the book for private rereading.

SELF-STIMULATION

It's not unusual to find children from six to nine years touching their genitals frequently, perhaps for prolonged periods of time. Again, the child is behaving in a completely normal, natural manner. But at this older age we may associate such masturbation with deliberate sexual action, and thus we may feel more uncomfortable with this behavior than earlier. How do we deal with it?

As always, a calm, casual approach is best. For if we say something like, "Nice boys (or girls) don't touch themselves there," the child may decide that particular area of the body must have something nasty about it. This can negatively affect sexual attitudes.

Perhaps we may notice self-stimulation occurring repeatedly. It may be an absentminded activity, such as when the child is watching television or is simply bored. In fact, many counselors believe that a child who lacks enough association with others and/or spends long periods of time alone is more likely to indulge in self-stimulation as a habit. Assuring ample participation with others—both inside and outside the family—will provide positive alternatives.

SETTING LIMITS

The six- to nine-year-old is becoming more responsible. As we allow privileges and set restrictions, consistency is essential so children know the limits. We parents needn't be uneasy about saying "No," if that's our well-considered action. Rather we should be cheerful but firm, explain our reasoning, and resolve to help our children gradually learn to deal with increasing freedom, as they demonstrate their ability to handle it. After all, that's one of the tasks of parenthood.

FACING THE CHALLENGE OF PARENTHOOD

Many parents looking back over the years think they would like another chance—that they would be wiser the second time around. The challenge of parenthood is enormous, yet we can accept it with complete confidence, even knowing we'll make countless mistakes over the years. How?

—By daily asking God's guidance and trusting His will for our lives
—By entrusting our children's development to His care rather than simply to our own knowledge and skill
—By telling our children over and over that we love them
—By demonstrating love through frequent gestures of affection ("Have you hugged your kid today?")
—By liberally praising their efforts (As one mother puts it, "One pat on the back is worth a dozen pats on the rear!")
—By accepting them as unique creations of God and trusting Him to round off the rough edges

QUESTIONS PARENTS ASK

Explaining Intercourse to a Grade-Schooler

My grade-schooler knows about reproduction, but I guess I should explain about sexual intercourse. How detailed should I get?

Answer: Children in the lower grades usually have only a passing interest in sex. However, somewhere along the way they're sure to pick up some information (usually faulty); and since they're not yet self-conscious about it, they'll probably come to you with frank questions.

It's assumed that you've already given your child basic information, including correct names for body parts. Still the child may have only a hazy memory of what you said or may merely need to hear it repeated. Listen to the question and answer honestly. Don't proceed with a long discussion for every simple question.

A young child may observe pets mating (which, by the way, is good background) and ask, "Do men and women ever do anything like that? Is that how people get a baby?"

Answer casually, something like this: "Those animals are mating. At certain times animals have the urge to mate, and they may mate with many different animals during that period. God made people different, though. He gave us love for each other, not just feelings called instincts. When a husband and wife want to have a baby or perhaps when they want to show that they love each other very much, they have what's called sexual intercourse. When they're all alone and feeling really close, the husband puts his penis into his wife's vagina. It's a very special thing, just between the husband and the wife."

A child this age may just say "Oh" and go out to play. Or the next remark may be "Yuk!" or something like, "Do they like it? Does it hurt?" You may even get questions such as, "Did you and Daddy do that to get me? Do you ever do it now?"

Again, answer matter-of-factly, something like: "When two grown people love each other, it doesn't hurt and they like it very much. Yes, that *is* how you began—with a tiny part from Mommy called an ovum or egg and a tiny part from Daddy called a sperm. When these two met, they formed one cell inside Mommy's body and you started to grow inside Mommy's uterus—a special place where you could be safe and warm until you were big enough to live on your own.

"When God made men and women, He gave them this way to show they love each other. So the answer to your question is 'Yes.' Daddy and I have intercourse, because we care about each other very much."

Letting children know that parents have sexual feelings—treating them as a natural part of living—assures youngsters that sexual expression is a normal ingredient in life. They'll mentally file this knowledge. It will help them cope with their own sexual feelings in coming years.

Your child may well ask random questions—one today and another six months from now. Take such questions in stride, answer them honestly, and enjoy this stage of your child's life. Because children don't yet personalize sexual information, this is a great opportunity to lay a strong, solid foundation for the healthy attitudes of a lifetime.

Try to appreciate the openness of this age. In a short while you'll be wishing you knew what was going on in your teenager's mind!

Exhibitionism

There's a man in our neighborhood who's an exhibitionist. How can I prepare my daughter, in case he should confront her?

Answer: The exhibitionist gets sexual gratification from exhibiting his genitals to unsuspecting observers. The typical case is a man who delights in showing himself to young girls. Obviously this is not normal behavior, but at least your child is not in physical danger. Most remain a safe distance away from their victims, and exposing themselves is their sole activity.

Such people are often called "flashers," and they *hope* to shock their viewers. Therefore any female confronted by a flasher is well-advised to act as though she's ignoring the entire performance. An older woman might choose to simply tell such a person he obviously needs psychological help.

Impress on your daughter that such a male is, indeed, sick and needs help. Reassure her that he won't harm her—that she'll probably be surprised and a bit frightened but is in no danger. After all, you may tell her, it's no big deal to see body parts. If she can see the situation as rather silly, it will help. And if she can feel pity for the exhibitionist who must get his kicks from such behavior, she'll probably be fine. (Of course you'll want to help the exhibitionist by reporting his behavior to the police.)

Child Abuse and Incest

I hear a lot about child abuse and incest these days. How can I let my child know about it without imparting fright?

Answer: Most sexual child abuse is with a member of the child's own family (incest)—an uncle, a sibling, a grandfather, a father or stepfather, a cousin. Typically it's an older male with a young female.

Such activity can occur at any time, long before the girl's body begins to develop, and may continue over a period of years. Most girls don't tell anyone about it—because they love the person involved, because they don't want to make him and/or their mother angry, because they've been threatened, etc. But they know instinctively that something is wrong, so they begin to feel ashamed, responsible in some vague, nameless fashion. And they almost always turn that guilt in upon themselves. This can cause later emotional and spiritual problems.

(Young boys are also subject to abuse, mostly from men or older boys who may or may not be related.)

It's important to give a child some guidelines, yet avoid instilling fear or suspicion: "Your body belongs to you. People may shake your hand or hug you or kiss you or pat you on the back, and that's fine because that's how we show you we love you! Or sometimes you may go to the doctor and he has to check you over from head to foot, and that's okay because that's his job.

"But other people shouldn't touch you around your vagina (penis). So if anyone ever does try to touch you there, get away from that person and come and tell me. I promise not to get angry with you. I want you to know that you can tell me *anything*."

8. Ten to Fourteen: Growing Up

Even a child shows what he is by what he does.

Proverbs 20:11 TEV

Your child is growing up. You can see it happening right before your eyes. "It seems like yesterday that Jana was a baby," says Becky wistfully. "Now she's 12 and losing her baby fat, developing a womanly shape. Her personality seems to be changing too. Sometimes she's so grown-up and responsible I say to myself, 'All those years of hard work are paying off.' I can really get a glimpse of the lovely young woman I hope she'll become. I'm proud of her—and of myself, I guess, because I think I've been a pretty fair parent.

"But then she'll turn around and do something so childish I can't believe it!"

Most parents of youngsters in the 10 to 14 age group can identify with Becky's feelings. These are years of rapid growth and change. Even the previously most stable, well-balanced youngsters become unpredictable. Parents are seldom prepared for this emotionally, even when warned. It's a time when parents need faith—not only in God but also in their children.

Underneath the turmoil, however, we can understand what's happening. Our children, though often puzzling and/or frustrating to us, have not really become strangers, haven't actually changed so much. What we see now are the temporary changes that are part of adolescence. The foundation we've been laying so carefully over the years is still there, whether plainly visible or not. And it can be continually reinforced by our prayers.

THE TIME OF AWAKENING

From ages 10 to 14 the child's own sense of sexuality is stirring. This is the age when many girls have intense friendships with other girls and boys with boys. But girls have begun to look at boys with interest, and boys are thinking someday soon they just might want to get close to someone soft and feminine—someone besides their mothers. As one 12-year-old boy put it, "If I ever stop hating girls, she'll be the first one on the list!"

This can be an unsettling time for young people. Their level of hormone production is changing rapidly, and emotions fluctuate greatly. All sorts of surprising things are happening to their bodies too, like the growth of hair under their arms and in the pubic area.

Girls note, usually with satisfaction, that their breasts are rounding. Some are upset to notice only one breast swelling (almost always a temporary condition) and may wonder whether they'll ever be "normal." The shape of the girl's hips changes, and she has her first menstrual period. And if she seems obsessed with her breasts and hips—continually wondering why one or the other can't be larger or smaller—relax! She's just a typical adolescent girl. But she needs your assurance that she's attractive as she is, that her body is just right for her.

Boys' bodies are changing too, although it may be less noticeable. A boy may be dismayed to see his breasts swelling and/or the nipples hardening. (He needs reassurance that it's normal and won't last long, even if he doesn't ask about it.) He's embarrassed to discover his penis gets stiff at times, and he may begin to have nocturnal emissions (wet dreams), probably around age 13. His voice may change.

Youngsters of both sexes are often depressed to find acne blemishing their formerly smooth complexions. This, of course, is usually due to the fluctuating hormonal levels and will settle down once that's stabilized. To make matters worse, young people have all sorts of thoughts that simultaneously frighten, intrigue, and please them.

What's a parent to do? Prepare them well in advance for these normal, natural body processes. Knowing what's happening to them— and why—will lessen many anxieties. But take it one step further. For example, boys should be told about menstruation, and girls should also hear the facts about boys. Girls need reassurance, too, that increased white vaginal discharge is normal. They should also be prepared *early* for menstruation. Today it's not uncommon for nine- and ten-year-olds to begin menstruating, and the average age of onset is in the 11-year-old range. The young girl whose first knowledge of menstruation comes when she discovers blood on her panties can be thoroughly frightened and bewildered.

TALKING ABOUT SEX

Unfortunately, parent-child communication about sexual matters often ceases during these years, just when it's needed most. "I get all tongue-tied. I know what I should say, but I can't get the words out," said one mother. "I keep thinking that perhaps I'll just give the children ideas," said a father. "Maybe I'm wrong, but I wonder whether they should hear all that stuff now. You know what they say—'Ignorance is bliss.'"

But ignorance is *not* bliss. When parents fail to communicate information and their own values, their children simply go elsewhere. They ask their friends, they avidly watch television and movies, and they may read dirty books. So we parents have to weigh our own awkwardness in talking with our children against the misinformation and distorted values they'll almost surely gather elsewhere.

Good books can be helpful here. *Sex and the New You*, Book Four in the Learning about Sex series, talks frankly about bodily changes and immediate concerns of this age group.

Such a book can provide an opening for conversation, once the child has read it. Or it may serve as a good follow-up, to reinforce knowledge gained during parent-child communication. But *no* book is an adequate substitute for heart-to-heart talks with a loving parent.

During such conversations it's well to be frank about our own feelings. "It's silly, I know, but I was petrified when I finally got up the courage to talk to my oldest daughter," confessed Christine. "I wasn't covering my discomfort very well, so finally I just admitted it. I explained that I was self-conscious because I'd never been able to talk to Grandma and Grandpa when I was young—and I really wanted to talk with her. Somehow that broke down the barriers on both sides, and from then on it was much easier for both of us."

When talking with our children, we'll want to answer questions about sex with absolute honesty. If a particular question stumps you, say, "I don't know the answer, but let's find out together." Don't mention only body parts, but talk also about your feelings about your own sexuality. Speak of your personal values, how love is expressed in family relationships—between husband and wife, by establishing your home, and by loving and caring for your children. Try to convey that sexuality is a gift from God and not to be abused. If you feel uncomfortable, admit it and forge ahead.

CLASSES ARE NOT ENOUGH

Some parents believe school sex education classes are all a young person needs. Not true! Such classes are often just discussions of body functions and personal hygiene. What about moral values? Thus your child may know all about sexual intercourse—may even have received a handbook on it—but have little knowledge of its effect on a young person's life. Some may have an understanding of contraception but may also have the impression that birth control makes sexual intercourse "safe" and harmless.

Youngsters may think of pregnancy or fathering a child as something that happens only to someone else—or only after prolonged periods of sexual intercourse. They may know the medical facts about abortion, but not the spiritual and psychological implications.

THEY'RE NOT TOO YOUNG TO KNOW!

And if we think our children are too young to hear such things at 11 or 12 or 13, we're only kidding ourselves. Youngsters that age—and younger—are engaging in sexual activity and becoming parents. Nor are these occurrences restricted to slum areas or to the big cities.

Also, if we haven't done so before, this is an excellent time to establish an open-door policy for our children's friends. Interaction with others is always helpful, and what better place for it than in our own home? Church youth groups usually offer opportunity for wholesome group participation.

"Phil and I have always dropped whatever we were doing to see that our kids got to the youth group activities at church. And we do whatever we can to help," remarked Patti. "The group isn't perfect, of course, but at least we know where they are and what they're hearing. Just to spend time with other Christian kids and to feel they are part of our church family has to be a good influence—and every little bit helps!"

DEALING WITH SELF-STIMULATION—AGAIN

Statistics tell us that most young people of this age masturbate. Why do they do it? Simply because it's pleasurable—and especially so now that the young person is experiencing newly developing sexual feelings. *Part* of the "cause" of masturbation, then, may be the desire to experiment, to discover more about one's burgeoning sexual development.

Recognizing that most young people overcome this habit as they mature, you'll want to be careful that you do not overreact. A harsh, shaming approach can do more harm than good—particularly if it becomes simply a matter of "laying down the Law."

Young people may have heard the myths of dreadful consequences of self-stimulation—like insanity or growing hair on the palms of their hands. Or they might wonder whether they're some kind of "pervert."

Thus you'll want to assure your young person that there is no evidence that self-stimulation causes any *physical* harm. Persistent, compulsive masturbation, however, can be the symptom of a deeper psychological and spiritual problem. It may be a way for the young person to cope with feelings of inadequacy, loneliness, rejection. It's *difficult* to learn how to relate to persons of the other sex, to deal with the awkwardness and the many tensions and uncertainties that go with first dating. Masturbation can become one way to cope.

Thus it's important that we parents be sympathetic listeners, seeking first to understand the pain which underlies persistent masturbation. Chances are great that the Christian young person is already feeling shame and guilt, particularly about the lustful sexual fantasies which usually go with masturbation. Our sympathetic understanding will help our young person to surface the guilt—and to hear again the good news of God's forgiveness.

TELL THEM ABOUT VD? VERY DEFINITELY!

Many parents are surprised to learn that gonorrhea is epidemic among junior high students. Nor is it confined to juvenile delinquents or young people from problem homes.

For example, the school nurse from a small Midwestern town described one case involving a 12-year-old girl with gonorrhea. She had interviewed the parents and the girl and found them to be a close, loving family with apparently high morals, living in a comfortable, middle class home—seemingly the ideal environment for raising children. Yet authorities had already uncovered 36 contacts relating to this one 12-year-old girl, and the investigation was not yet complete.

COPING WITH THE CHANGES

As any parent knows, young people often seem to undergo a complete personality change. They may act amazingly adult at times and minutes later throw a temper tantrum like a three-year-old or revert to a whining, frightened child in need of comfort. Although trying, these abrupt mood swings are a normal part of the development process.

Youngsters may also seem determined to avoid as much contact with family members as possible. "When Lisa was 13, she became a sort of hermit around here," said Lorna. "I think she spent most of that year and part of the next up in her room! She'd come down for meals—reluctantly. Then just as surely as the sun rises in the east, one of us would make some remark that would set her off. She'd dash for the stairs, slam every door loudly and vanish again. Honestly, none of us could say or do anything right!"

Lisa's behavior pattern was not unusual, and most youngsters pass through it on their own timetable.

LET THEM KNOW THEY'RE OKAY

Unfortunately, the child's grown-up look may make either or both parents uncomfortable. Parents may think they shouldn't touch their children anymore, that perhaps it's "wrong." Yet a hug, a pat on the back, positive assurances such as, "You're really a nice person and I love you" are exactly what the developing adolescent needs. Such frequent, genuine gestures affirm our youngsters' feelings of acceptability as persons, in spite of their own nagging self-doubt.

Our adolescent children need our approval more than ever. Besides their own fears and insecurities, the climate in which young people operate is often one of continuing putdowns by their peers. Even good friends may think it's extremely clever to be sarcastic—especially since it usually brings a laugh—at someone else's expense. There are young people who are expert surgeons; they know each person's weak spot and just how to dissect another's ego.

DEALING WITH LABELS

Another thing that many youngsters live with is the fear of being labeled homosexual. Some youngsters struggle with guilt feelings and uncertainty because of episodes of homosexual play. (Such behavior does occur, especially among young boys.) Also, males who are small for their age, who are slightly built or have a high-pitched voice, are often tagged as "fairies." A girl who appears boyish may be dubbed a "lez." If two girls walk hand-in-hand or two boys seem friendly, they may well be teased about being "homos" or "fags."

This effectively ensures that friends keep their distance, that young people try to act so there won't be any doubt about their sexual nature, perhaps purposely adopting a belligerent manner. But if their physical characteristics cast them into a mold, how can they escape? That's why it's important to reassure them that their bodies are developing according to their own individual timetables. If such a growth pattern is a family characteristic, or if a parent has had similar feelings, it helps them to hear of it.

For instance, when Craig saw his son moping around the house, refusing to go out and play ball with the gang, he suspected the reason. "You know, Eric, when I was your age I had a terrible time. I was the runt of my class. The guys in my P. E. class acted like I had the plague or something. It seemed I could never throw a ball right—or do anything else right, for that matter. And the girls, well, they totally ignored me. There I was, 14, and I looked about 10! Even when Grandpa told me that all the Meyer men had been built like me when they were my age, it didn't help one bit.

"But you know what? The year I was a junior in high school I grew a foot, put on 30 pounds . . ."

Craig's remarks helped his son to accept his body—to feel okay about himself. But there's the opposite problem, too; there's the girl who develops earlier than her contemporaries and is "really built." Such a girl has her own difficulties, for she is almost inevitably labeled "hot." The boys make suggestive remarks, and the other girls (who are envious and on different timetables) spin wild tales. And although it happens less frequently, an early developing boy can experience similar problems.

COMPARISONS CAN BE HARMFUL

Although parents can be helpful as Craig was, they can also damage their children's self-image through thoughtless remarks and constant comparisons with others. "My mom had one strategy when I was growing up—and I hated it!" said Mindy. "When my friends were around she'd say something like, 'Mindy, *when* are you going to stop being so clumsy?' or 'Don't go into Mindy's room—it looks like a pigpen!' My friends would laugh, but I'd be dying inside.

"Or she'd praise my sister, who was a brain, and ask, 'Why can't you be more like Stephanie? You're just as smart as she is. Obviously, you just don't study as hard.' Teachers said the same thing, year after year.

"But if the plan was to make me work harder, it backfired. I just resented all of them—Mom for ridiculing and nagging me all the time and poor Steph for her good grades. And I hated myself most of all, because I saw myself as a loser who would never measure up."

A far better course of action is when we frequently tell our children it's okay to be different—that in fact we rejoice in their individuality and they should, too. If we can instill in them the solid conviction that God made them as they are, that there never has been nor ever will be someone just like them—that God has a plan for using their strengths and weaknesses, many potential problems of later life will never appear.

A CLIMATE FOR GROWTH

Establishing an atmosphere where we can speak comfortably about sexual concerns will help our children know they are free to come to us for advice and answers. Surely that's what we want, isn't it, even if it makes us a bit uneasy at times?

All this is part of raising children to become well-adjusted adults. One psychologist says, "Wise parents work themselves out of a job." Our goal is young adults who have a God-pleasing set of values, healthy attitudes, and the ability to govern themselves.

There are times when that seems an impossible task because we're well aware of our failures and weaknesses. We can't do it on our own!

So we pray for God's guidance and forgiveness, and we trust Him to use even our mistakes.

QUESTIONS PARENTS ASK

R-Rated Movies

My children say I'm old-fashioned because I don't want them to see R-rated movies. Should I exert any control over which movies my kids see?

Answer: Many concerned parents make it a policy never to let their youngsters view any movie unless they've seen it themselves or have a recommendation from someone they trust. (Not an easy task!) There are also rating guides in many magazines for parents.

Talk it over with your child, explaining why you object to a particular movie or television program. Talk about your values as a Christian family. Don't moralize and lecture. Once your youngster is old enough to date or drive, of course, you'll have less control.

Yes, watching R-rated movies and suggestive or violent TV programming can influence young people. Studies show that heavy viewers of television and movies, both children and adults, tend to be more fearful about life in general. They also more readily accept abnormal behavior and deviant life-styles as the norm. In other words, they begin to perceive life as portrayed on the screen or the tube rather than as it's lived by the average person.

We're all influenced by what we watch and read. It's a bit like that computer slogan—GIGO. That translates to "garbage in—garbage out." If true of computers, it's also true of the human mind.

Menstruation

When and how can I tell my daughter about menstruation?

Answer: Girls should be told about menstruation by the age of nine, simply because more and more girls are beginning to have their menstrual cycles by this age. And certainly the girl whose body is developing *must* be told. The girl who suddenly begins to bleed from her vagina and hasn't been prepared for it may fear she has an injury. She may feel ashamed to tell anyone—even a beloved teacher—about it, so she may experience a great deal of needless anxiety.

You'll find the process described in Book Three of this series, *How You Are Changing*, by Jane Graver. You will find this book very helpful. The companies that manufacture sanitary napkins also have excellent illustrated booklets available. In any case, don't wait for your daughter to ask. Pick a time when you think you're communicating well on other levels, and then just begin.

You may wish to say something like this: "You're growing up fast, and soon you'll be an adult. Your body will go through many changes—changes that will prepare you to be an adult and to be a mother someday if you wish. One of the earliest signs may come when you notice a thick, white discharge on your panties. That means your body is maturing and getting ready for menstruation (men-stroo-A-shun). All girls menstruate. Some begin when they're about your age, a few earlier, and some much later. Some may begin as late as 18. No one knows exactly when each girl will have her first menstrual period.

"You have seen ads for feminine protection products on television (name some currently being advertised). Those products are for a woman when she is having her menstrual period.

"It all begins with a part of your body called the pituitary gland. That gland controls your personal timetable. You may notice soon that you or some of your girlfriends are beginning to get hair under the arms and between the legs. Your breasts may begin to swell, and your waist will narrow down. These are all signs that your body is getting ready for you to become an adult woman.

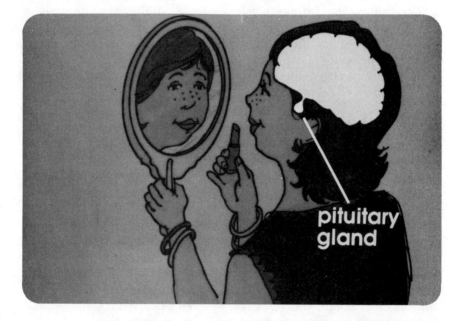

pituitary gland

"God created females so that each of us has all the equipment we need to be a woman: two ovaries, two fallopian tubes, a uterus, and a vagina. (Show diagram if possible.) Your ovaries are filled with thousands of ova (also known as egg cells), which are the female reproductive cells. Those cells make it possible for you to have a baby someday if you choose.

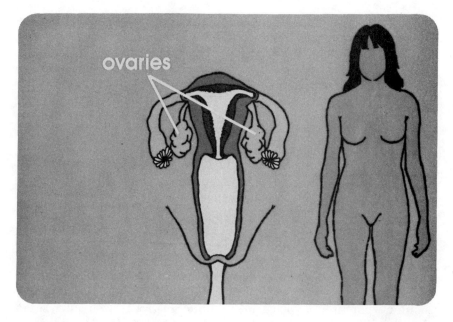

"One day, when the pituitary gland signals that your body is ready, hormones will travel to your ovaries and tell them to get started doing their job. In about two weeks an egg cell leaves the ovary (called ovulation) and new hormones are secreted. These cause the blood and cells inside the walls of the uterus to swell.

"If the egg is fertilized by a sperm (the male cell), this rich new lining will provide a good place for the egg to fasten and begin to grow

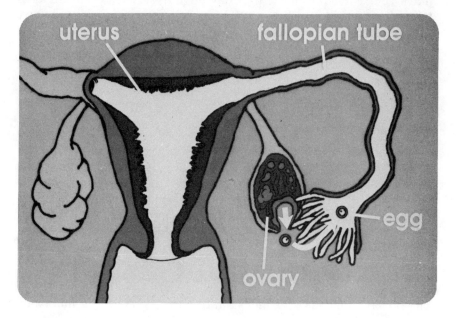

into a baby. Most of the time, though, the egg is *not* fertilized, and the uterus gets rid of this lining of old blood and cells.

"So your body must clean house. The old blood and cells from the uterus must leave the body. This is called the menstrual flow. It comes out through the natural passageway God designed—the vagina. The menstrual flow continues for about three to five days, and then it's all over for another month until your ovaries release another egg. Once it starts, your body will continue this regular cycle over and over for about 30 years, unless you become pregnant or ill.

"For most girls, menstrual periods are not painful. Most girls can go on doing everything they always do. Some girls get a little twinge or a slight cramp in their abdomen once in a while, but doctors say the best thing to do for that is to get some exercise—whatever you enjoy doing at other times.

"One of these days you'll go to the bathroom and you'll notice blood on the toilet paper or on your panties. That's like your body announcing to you that it's getting ready to be a grown-up body. If it happens at school, you can ask the school nurse or your (female) teacher for a sanitary napkin. If you're in a public restroom, you may see a dispenser on the wall where you can drop in a coin and buy a sanitary napkin. Of course, if it happens here at home you can come to me.

"Here, I'll show you how to use a sanitary pad so you'll know what to do. And I've bought you your very own box to keep on your closet shelf, just in case I'm not here when you need them.

"In the beginning your periods may be irregular. After a while they will usually come about every 28 to 30 days. It's a good idea to mark your calendar on the first day of your period so you can keep track. Then you'll remember to take a pad with you in case you start your period away from home.

"You'll also learn quickly how often you need to change your sanitary napkin. Other than changing your pad regularly, the only thing to remember is to bathe or shower frequently so that you feel fresh and dainty."

Note to Mothers

Remember (again) that more is caught than taught. If your daughter observes you displaying negative attitudes during your own menstrual period—if you call menstruation "the curse," etc.—she will absorb and adopt the same attitude. In fact, many authorities believe most menstrual problems are caused more by psychological difficulties (often attitudes learned from one's mother) than by actual physical problems.

How old should a girl be before she begins to use a tampon?

Answer: If a girl has been menstruating for six months or more and her body is normal, she should have no trouble. Explain that the tampon is a pack of absorbent cotton or gauze attached to a string, which is inserted into the vagina to absorb the menstrual flow. Assure her that no harm comes from inserting a tampon into the vagina and that it is not painful—unless she is nervous or frightened and thus tightens the muscles at the vaginal entrance. If a girl has a good attitude and remains relaxed, a little practice should make insertion and removal simple. Most brands have an instruction leaflet in each box.

Your physician will be happy to answer any questions regarding the use of tampons or other sanitary protection.

Should boys be told about menstruation?

Answer: Yes, boys should be given the same basic information at about the same age. In particular, emphasize that the menstrual cycle is a normal and natural part of the female life. It's also good for a boy to understand that if a girl declines sports activity or the like, he should accept her decision without expecting a long explanation.

Explaining the Gynecological Exam

My adolescent daughter is due for a complete physical exam. I remember how embarrassed and frightened I was the first time I had a gynecological checkup. How can I prepare my daughter?

Answer: Talk it through with your daughter so she knows what to expect. You may wish to say something like this: "Now that you're growing up, the doctor needs to check and make sure that your body is developing normally. So he may want to do a vaginal examination. He'll tell you to take your panties off and to cover yourself with a large cloth. Or perhaps he may tell you to take off all your clothes and put on a gown. Either way, he'll leave the examining room while you're changing clothes, but the nurse may help you.

"When he comes back in, he should check your breasts, too. This is an important part of a regular exam for a female, just to make sure everything is okay. He will give you literature on self breast examination and explain the procedure. Next he or the nurse will tell you to put your feet into the holders on the sides of the table and to scoot down. You'll be covered with a sheet, but you'll probably think the whole thing must look pretty ridiculous with your knees sticking up in the air. And you'll be right, because it is rather undignified! But it makes it easier for the doctor to examine you.

"Next the doctor may move a light closer, and he'll most likely insert a metal instrument into your vagina. You won't feel anything except a cold sensation. The doctor uses the instrument to spread the

69

lips of the vagina apart so that he can see more easily. He'll look inside, and he may also insert a finger (he'll be wearing rubber gloves) so that he can feel if everything is as it should be. He may also press on your tummy sometime during the examination.

"To do the 'Pap' test he'll take a long cotton swab and get a sample of the cells present in the cervix (mouth of the uterus). This will be smeared on a piece of glass and sent to a laboratory for examination. Now that you're growing up, you'll have regular 'Pap' tests, because it's an important way to make sure that everything is normal.

"That's usually all there is to it. It would be a lot easier, of course, if a female's reproductive system weren't all inside the body, but that's the way God made us. Getting a gynecological exam is a routine thing for women of all ages. It doesn't hurt, so just try and be relaxed.

"Perhaps you're wondering what the doctor thinks about all this. Well, doctors see all parts of the body all day, every day, day after day. When they examine a female, they're just looking for signs of problems and checking for the way various membranes look and that sort of thing. They don't think of it as a male touching a female; it's just part of their responsibility to help people stay well.

"Like any other new experience, having an exam may make you feel a bit self-conscious or embarrassed, but that's all right. Soon you'll feel at ease about it. And all of us need to take good care of these marvelous bodies God gave us. The vagina and uterus are very important parts of our body, and we want to do everything we can to keep them healthy. And always remember: You are the physician's patient, and you should feel free to ask questions not only then but at any time you need help in clarifying physical problems."

Note to Mothers

A young girl may be uncomfortable if left alone in the examining room with a male doctor. You have a right to remain in the room with your daughter if she prefers. Or she may want to have only the nurse present. Either way, make sure your daughter knows she can make her requests known. If necessary *you* take the initiative and insist upon it so this exam turns out to be a positive experience for her.

Nocturnal Emissions

How should a boy be prepared for nocturnal emissions (wet dreams)?

Answer: A casual explanation of nocturnal emissions (preferably by the father or other close male—simply because he speaks from firsthand knowledge) should be given at about age 12, before they begin. If a mother has an open relationship with her son and feels comfortable talking with him about sexual matters, she can do the honors.

The son should be told that while he is dreaming—perhaps about girls—his penis may stiffen, allowing the urethra to straighten out. Then the semen, containing sperm, shoots out (ejaculation). There is no "normal" interval between wet dreams; for some boys it is days, for some weeks.

If a boy is not prepared in advance, the first time he wakes up and finds a whitish, sticky material on his bedclothes he may be totally bewildered. The color and consistency will tell him it's not urine—but what is it? He may be mortified and wonder what his mother will think when she washes his sheets. He may even think he is sick in some way.

Reassure him that this is a normal, healthy sign that his body is maturing, that he's getting ready to be a man. Also, either in this discussion or at another time, you'll want to point out that wet dreams are a sign he is physically able to father a child, although he is far from ready to *be* a father, with all that entails.

Don't be alarmed and assume that nocturnal emissions (no matter how frequent) mean your son is obsessed with sex. These occur during the dream state and are a natural way of draining off sexual tensions. Don't question him or ask what kind of dreams he had or make a big deal out of it in any way. Wet dreams are as natural for boys as menstruation is for girls.

(Normal adult men may also have nocturnal emissions, especially during times of prolonged abstinence.)

Should I explain nocturnal emissions to my daughter?

Answer: Yes, explain the process and caution her not to taunt her brother(s). Also emphasize that this is the male body's built-in method for taking care of sexual tensions. Therefore if a young man ever confronts your daughter with the argument that he *must* have intercourse or "he'll go crazy," she'll be aware that this is not true.

Explaining Sex to Preteens

I told my children the facts of life long ago. Now that they are ages 10 and 12, how much more should I say?

Answer: When talking to your 10- to 14-year-old about sex, present the basic general facts but personalize them to fit. You may wish to say something like this: "We've talked about sex before, but now that you're older you'll look at it differently than you did. Besides, you may have forgotten some of the terms, so let's go over it again.

"Here's a drawing of the body parts of the male body and the female body. (Show them the diagrams on pages 20, 21, and 22 of this book or those in *Love, Sex, and God*, Book Five in this series.) I'm sure you know

71

what a penis is—the male sexual organ. It's also the part of his body through which urine is eliminated. The body takes what it needs to stay healthy from the food we eat, then collects the wastes for elimination. The liquid waste, called urine, is collected in the bladder and passes out through the urethra, which is a hollow tube somewhat like a soda straw. A male's urethra is in his penis. A female's urethra is inside her body, and there's a small opening on the outside.

"A male also has testicles—two egg-shaped bodies which manufacture sperm. The sperm are male reproductive cells so tiny you need a microscope to see them. At your age a male's body is maturing so that he can father children. Sometimes he is puzzled when his penis suddenly gets stiff. This is called an erection. It sticks out, and he may feel embarrassed about it.

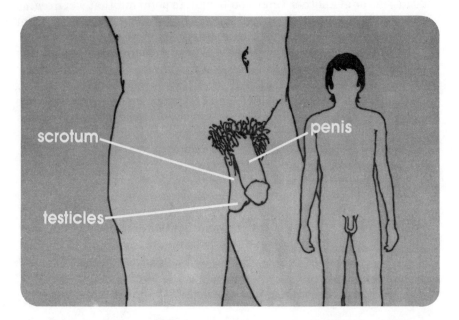

"Some boys find their breasts swelling a bit, and they may think they'll end up looking like a girl. But they won't—it's only a temporary thing and nothing to get self-conscious about. Sometimes a boy's nipples get hard, too. All these are signs that his body is getting ready for the day when he'll be ready to marry and perhaps have children.

"Because normal body temperature would destroy the sperm, God designed the testicles to be outside the body, inside a pouch of skin called the scrotum, where the temperature is a couple of degrees cooler. If a fellow should happen to bump his testicles or get kicked there when playing football, it would probably hurt a lot because there are many nerve endings concentrated there. That's why it's a good idea to protect the testicles and penis from injury.

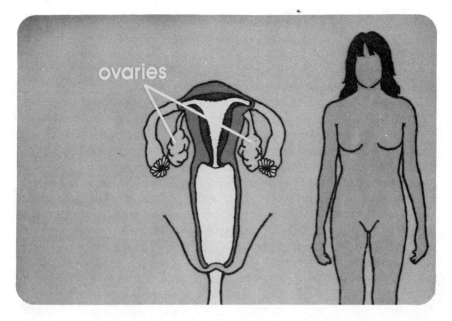

"You can see by the diagram that a female's reproductive system is all up inside her body." (When talking to a young girl it's well to add: "You might be curious to see what your own body looks like. It's not easy to look at yourself without a mirror. Sometime when you're alone you might want to compare your own body with the diagram so you'll know the names for the parts of your body." Young girls sometimes think "nice girls" don't look at themselves. Your suggestion will let her

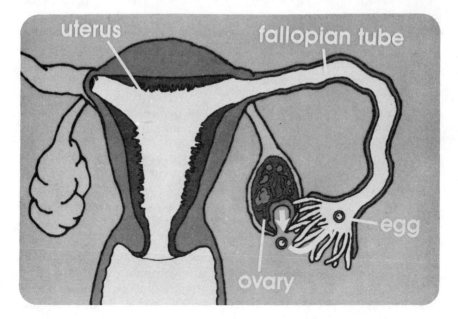

know it's okay.) "A female has two egg-shaped parts, too, called the ovaries. This is where the ova, or egg cells, are stored. Every girl is on her own timetable, so there's no exact age when it happens, but one day one of her ovaries will release an egg which will travel down the fallopian tubes to the uterus.

"The uterus has been getting ready for the egg, building up a thick lining of rich blood cells to nourish it, in case the egg cell has been joined by a male sperm, which we call fertilization, Most of the time it hasn't, so after a couple of weeks the unused blood cells just loosen and become the girl's monthly menstrual flow.

"If the egg cell had been fertilized, a baby would begin to grow in the uterus. At your age a girl's body is just going through the menstrual cycle to get ready for the day when she's ready for marriage and may want to have a baby. But once a girl begins to menstruate, it's *possible* for her to have a baby.

"Your body is growing and changing in many ways. You'll notice as you look at your friends that they come in all shapes and sizes. Some are short, some are tall. Some are fat, some are thin. Johnny, you've probably noticed that penises and testicles are different shapes and sizes, too. Perhaps you've wondered whether your penis is 'normal' size. (Mary, you may have worried that you're too flat in front—or too round in back.) You've probably noticed that girls come in all shapes and sizes. Some have been menstruating for awhile, yet others haven't even begun. But let's get one thing straight: God made each of us an individual, and that means we have our own schedule for growing up, too.

"You're also growing hair under your arms and between your legs—what's called the pubic area. Some people have a lot of pubic hair, others not much. It's meant as a protection for your sex organs and also to keep your skin from getting irritated by perspiration.

"And I've seen you frowning into the mirror at your pimples (acne). These are normal, too. You see, all these changes are happening because your hormone balance is changing from a child to an adult. It takes awhile to get everything balanced perfectly, so there will be times when your pimples will be worse. Your skin and hair are more oily, too, and you probably perspire more.

"All this is okay! Remember this: Each person is on a different schedule, so each one is normal for him or her. Wouldn't it be boring if we were all alike? There's never any need to worry, nor should you ever make fun of anyone else. It's all part of God's wonderful design when He made us male and female.

"That means He gave us our sexual nature, too. When a husband and wife are feeling very loving, they may want to touch each other—all over. They may want an extra-special way to show they really care about each other. One of those ways is called sexual intercourse. When they have these feelings about each other, the husband's penis begins to get hard and straight. The wife's vagina gets ready, too, by becoming softer and more relaxed and a bit slippery.

"As they lie close to each other, the husband puts his penis into the wife's vagina, in just the way God planned. They begin to move their bodies together, enjoying the pleasurable feelings it gives them. Soon the testicles release some sperm and the seminal fluid comes out through the penis and into the wife's vagina. This does not hurt the wife in any way. The name for this is ejaculation, and you should know that urine never comes out at the same time as the semen. After ejaculation the penis becomes smaller and softer.

"The wife doesn't ejaculate, of course. But she has the same good feelings as her husband. When sexual intercourse is over, the husband and wife enjoy the way they feel—warm and relaxed and very, very loving.

"A husband and wife enjoy having intercourse very much. Sooner or later they may want to have a baby, and this also begins with intercourse—and the union of the egg cell and the sperm. During ejaculation millions of sperm are released. The sperm are shaped like tiny commas, and they swim rapidly toward the fallopian tubes, trying to get to the egg cell, which is smaller than a dot. As soon as one has penetrated the tiny egg, no more sperm can penetrate it, and pregnancy has begun.

"Now the fertilized egg moves from the fallopian tube to the uterus. It attaches itself to the inside of the uterus. Remember when we talked about the rich lining of tissue containing many blood vessels which the uterus prepares each month? Well, those blood cells nourish the egg and help it get off to a good start. Within a very short time this one cell—the union of sperm and egg—will begin to divide and form two cells. The two divide into four and so on. This tiny cell is the beginning of a baby which will grow inside the woman's uterus. This is how you and I and everyone else on earth got here, and it's part of God's wonderful plan for men and women.

"Pretty soon you may begin to think you're grown-up and ready to have sexual intercourse—even to have a baby. Perhaps some of your friends are even bragging about having sex. But people have to be older and more responsible before they're ready for this kind of relationship. God designed sexual intercourse for husbands and wives. It's more than two bodies getting together. God meant for us to have a commitment to each other, most of all.

"Remember that Bible lesson you learned about Adam and Eve? That's when God said to Eve that she would have a desire toward her husband. That means that husbands and wives want to be close, to hold each other and show how much they love each other. They want to establish a home and become a family. And that's what God wants, too. People who accept less than that—like some of the characters on television or in the movies, who have intercourse with first one person and then another—are missing out on the best. They're settling for second-rate. And many times they mess up their whole lives."

Telling Youngsters About Pregnancy and Birth

How much do I tell my preteen about pregnancy and birth?

Answer: Youngsters this age are extremely curious about this subject. They want to know *everything*. Blessed indeed is the adolescent who can talk freely with understanding parents.

Answer questions honestly, calmly, casually, so your youngster absorbs the idea that this is a natural part of living. If you're stumped, admit it and promise to find the answer. Then do it.

Also, don't read great significance into the questions asked. A chance remark or something in the media may have aroused curiosity. Beware of pouncing with a WHY-do-you-want-to-know? attitude or you'll not get a second chance to have your child talk freely with you.

It's assumed your youngster knows the names of body parts and functions from previous conversations. However, it can be helpful to refer to a diagram of the human body and briefly review. Then you can be sure your child will understand the terminology.

You may wish to say something like this: "Sometimes a husband and wife may decide they want to have a baby. And we've talked before about how the egg cell from the wife and the sperm from the husband unite in the fallopian tube of the female. We say the egg cell has been fertilized by the sperm. This is the beginning of new life. This new cell then travels to the uterus (also called the womb) and begins to grow.

"Hair color, eye color, the shape of the nose and the mouth—all these and a bunch of other qualities, including the baby's sex, are determined at the instant of conception. Isn't that marvelous? Each new child is unique—a special person, with special talents and abilities. There never has been—and never will be—another human being just like you.

"After conception that tiny clump of new life fastens onto the inside of the female's uterus, which has been prepared with a soft, thick cushion of tissue with many small blood vessels filled with lots of rich, red blood cells to nourish the growing child. The mother's first hint that she's pregnant comes when she misses her regular menstrual period. After that there are special tests to make sure.

"The developing new life is called the embryo. Soon it's surrounded by fluid and enclosed in a membrane. What keeps the embryo alive and makes it grow? Well, it's attached to the wall of the uterus and gets its food and oxygen right from its mother's bloodstream. Wastes are eliminated in the same way. That means that when a pregnant woman eats a good diet the baby gets proper nourishment, too. But if she does

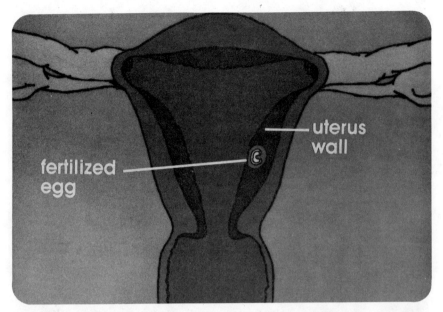

something harmful—if she takes drugs or drinks alcohol or eats poorly or smokes cigarettes—the baby takes in the same thing and may be harmed. For instance, it may not develop properly.

"The embryo—that bit of new life from the mother and the father—keeps growing and developing. After the eighth week it's called a fetus. By the fourth or fifth month the doctor can hear the baby's heartbeat with his stethoscope and the mother can feel the baby moving and kicking.

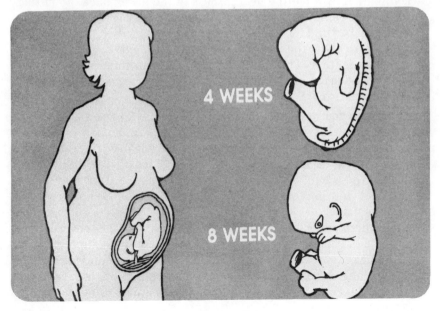

"The child keeps on growing and developing. The arms and legs and eyes and eyelashes and fingernails and hair and all the rest of the things a newborn baby has are forming. Finally, after about nine months the baby is ready to live on its own and the mother begins to feel the first signs of what is known as labor. That's her signal that it's about time for her baby to be born.

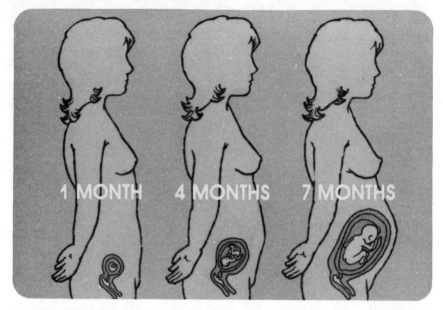

"Usually labor begins as a kind of cramping in the lower abdomen, accompanied by a feeling of tightness in the lower back. Soon these contractions begin to come at regular times as her body gets ready for the baby's birth. The opening to the uterus, called the cervix, is stretching to allow the baby to come out. The contractions get closer and closer together. The mother usually has a doctor or midwife there to help her with the birth, and most of the time she goes to the hospital when labor begins.

"Perhaps you're wondering whether it hurts for the mother's body to stretch like that. Most mothers have some pain, but if you ask them they usually say they didn't really mind because they knew the discomfort was accomplishing something. It was bringing their new baby into the world! It's a bit like when you're sore after running in a track meet; you don't mind the aching muscles because it was worth it to win the prize!

"The birth process is called delivery, and it may take several hours before the uterus has stretched enough to allow the baby to pass into the birth canal or vagina. But it's not as bad as it sounds because in between contractions the mother can just relax and she feels quite comfortable. Finally the baby is ready to make its appearance. The opening of the vagina must also stretch, and although you might think it couldn't possibly enlarge enough to allow a baby to pass through, you'd be wrong, because that's exactly what happens.

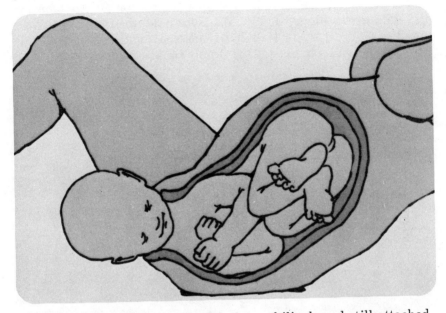

"And so the baby is born, with the umbilical cord still attached. Once the infant takes its first breath and its lungs inflate, the cord is not needed anymore, so it's cut and clamped—which doesn't hurt the baby. (Your navel or belly button shows where the umbilical cord used to be.) The child is then laid on the mother's breast so she can see and touch this little stranger she's been waiting for. The placenta and the sac that surrounded the baby come out of the vagina last, and then the mother's uterus and vaginal opening begin to get smaller. Soon they have returned almost to the exact size they were before she became pregnant.

"I remember how it was when *you* were born. We looked at you and were amazed that God could take that tiny bit from each of us and form it into you. You were God's gift to us. And we were very thankful that He watched over all of us.

"Like all new parents we looked you over very carefully. And we marveled that you could be a real, separate, living person—that you had blood vessels and a heart, lungs that could breathe, and a voice that could yell surprisingly loud! That reminded us of Psalm 139:13, 15-16, where it says:

> You created every part of me; You put me together in my mother's womb. . . . When my bones were being formed . . . when I was growing there in secret, You knew that I was there—You saw me before I was born (TEV).

"It really is a miracle from God, isn't it? But there's another miracle, too. After the baby's birth the mother's breasts begin to fill with milk. The baby is born with the instinct to suck, so it knows what to do. And usually a mother has just enough milk for her own baby. As the child grows bigger and drinks more milk, the mother's breasts produce a larger supply. If she had twins, she would have enough milk for them, too. You might say the supply equals the demand.

"Are you wondering whether it hurts the mother when the baby nurses? The answer is no. Sometimes for the first few days her breasts may be a bit tender. But a mother feels so good that she can give her child what's needed that the tiny bit of discomfort doesn't bother her. After a week or two both she and the baby feel like old pros. Later, when the baby gets older, the mother may decide it's time to start giving milk from a cup or a bottle. And then her breasts stop producing milk and get smaller, as they were before she got pregnant.

"You may notice that some mothers always feed their babies from a bottle. There may be a problem or some other reason why they choose to use a bottle. But they hold their babies close and love them just as much as the mothers who breastfeed, and the babies are healthy, too. It all depends on what the parents and the doctor think is best.

"You're old enough to know that sometimes people have babies under other circumstances, such as when a teenage girl isn't married and has a child. Such a mother may still love her child, but it's much harder because she feels all alone. And God really meant for children to be born and live in families, where there are parents who are able to support themselves and care for the children.

"Of course, there are all kinds of families. Some homes may have just a mother, some just a father. Maybe one parent has died or the parents have been divorced. That doesn't mean kids can't be happy in such a home. It just means the parent has to work harder at the job and everybody in the family has to pull together even more. Because that's what a family is—people who love each other and care about each other and help each other."

Rape

How do I tell my daughter about rape? How can I help her protect herself?

Answer: The most important thing you can impress on your daughter is that rape is *not*, as most people think, related to sex. Rather it's a crime of violence and rage. The rapist wants to act out his hate. A female, being physically weaker, becomes the "logical" target.

Rape doesn't happen because of a female's clothes or the way she walks. It's just that she's there—and the rapist wants to hurt her. She may be three or 83, it makes no difference.

Because of this growing problem most major cities now have rape crisis centers where victims can get sympathetic medical care and counseling. Females should be encouraged to contact this service in case of need—*before* they do anything else such as take a shower or change clothes.

All of us—women and men alike—must stop associating shame with the victim of rape. The shame and guilt should rest on the rapist, not the victim. For in spite of all the old jokes, an attacker who holds a switchblade at one's throat or who threatens with a gun, who is bigger and physically stronger—and powerfully determined as well—can force a female to submit. At that moment she can't be sure the sick-minded man who promises to slit her throat is not serious. For most victims, submitting is equated with simple survival.

We should warn even our young daughter about being cautious and teach her some simple safety guidelines. (Contact your local public library, police station, or rape crisis center for more information.) But it's important to keep a balanced perspective. We don't want her to fear every male she sees. Our goal should rather be a healthy respect for hazardous situations and an attitude of sensible caution. And we'll want to emphasize again and again that our daughter can tell us *anything*.

Transvestites and Transsexuals

My kids saw something on television the other day and asked me all about transvestites and transsexuals. Help!

Answer: The term *transvestite* means cross-dressing. The typical transvestite is male but is not a homosexual. He enjoys dressing in clothes of the opposite sex. Some like to wear one item of feminine attire such as a bra or panties under their own regular clothing—perhaps at all times or just once in a while. Others enjoy dressing entirely in women's clothing, using makeup, etc. This may be an occasional act or it may be a masquerade that endures lifelong.

The majority of transvestites have normal heterosexual relationships, are married and father children. The wife may or may not be aware of her husband's cross-dressing. Transvestites do not wish to change their sex or to have hormones or surgery. They want to be left alone and allowed to indulge their desire to wear female clothing whenever they feel the urge.

A *transsexual* is usually a male. His psychological orientation is so thoroughly that of the other sex that he views his sex organ as a deformity. His body is that of the normal male, but in his mind he's totally female. He wants to live the life of a woman and to engage in a *heterosexual* relationship with another man.

In recent years more and more transsexuals have undergone hormone therapy and/or sex-change surgery. The hormones cause the breasts to develop, facial hair to soften and lessen, and the voice to rise in pitch. Because sex-change surgery is so drastic, most doctors require the transsexual to undergo appropriate hormone therapy and in-depth counseling for a considerable time before the necessary surgical procedures. Surgery involves removal of the testicles and penis, leaving enough skin to form an artificial vagina.

QUESTIONS KIDS ASK

Can Every Couple Have a Baby?

Can every couple have a baby if they want to?

Answer: The answer is no. Sometimes the wife's reproductive organs didn't form right or she may have a health problem of some kind. Or the husband may have a low sperm count. That means either his semen contains fewer than average numbers of sperm or that the sperm are weak. But most couples have no difficulty in having children of their own.

Artificial Insemination

I heard that sometimes a woman can go to a doctor and he puts some sperm inside her. What is that called?

Answer: Artificial insemination. Sperm is collected from the husband and placed inside the wife's vagina with a medical instrument. If one of the sperm fertilizes her egg cell, pregnancy will result.

What is a test-tube baby?

Answer: Under laboratory conditions, the husband's sperm is added to an ovum from the wife. If fertilized, the new cell is placed into the uterus. If the fertilized ovum attaches itself to the wall of the uterus, pregnancy results.

Adoption

Why don't people just adopt a baby if they can't have one of their own?

Answer: Many couples want to adopt a baby more than anything, but there aren't enough babies available. Nowadays lots of unmarried mothers choose to raise their babies alone rather than allow them to be placed with a childless couple for adoption. So a couple may have to wait several years before they will have a chance to adopt.

People who are able to adopt a child love their child very, very much. After all, they wanted a child for so long before they got one! They feel just like other parents—they're proud of their child, they worry sometimes, and they scold sometimes. But mostly they just love their child and thank God for this youngster they waited so long to have!

Premature Babies

What does it mean when a baby is premature?

Answer: It simply means that the baby was born early—after six, seven, or eight months instead of the normal nine months. That almost always means there will be some problems. The lungs, for example, may not be fully developed for the baby to breathe properly. Hospitals are equipped to take care of such infants, and they have a lot of special equipment to help keep the baby alive until it can get along well on its own.

Miscarriage

What happens if a baby is born way too early—like at four or five months?

Answer: After the 16th week this is called a miscarriage. Before that it's called a spontaneous abortion. Both happen unintentionally, and the reasons aren't always clear. The baby is seldom able to live on its own.

More Boys or Girls

Are there more boy babies or girl babies born?

Answer: There are about 105 males born for every 100 females. Doctors aren't quite sure why this is true.

What Determines Sex?

How does a baby get to be a boy or a girl, anyhow?

Answer: All cells contain chromosomes which contain genes, which pass on traits you inherit, like blue eyes or red hair. There are 22 pairs of chromosomes that determine the inherited characteristics. But the 23rd pair of chromosomes is the one that decides what sex the child will be. Every female ovum contains an X chromosome. The ovum is fertilized by the male sperm, which may contain *either* an X chromosome or a Y chromosome. If the pair is XX, the child will be a girl; if XY, the child will be a boy.

Predicting Sex of Fetus

Can you tell whether a baby will be a boy or a girl before it's born?

Answer: There are some fairly new procedures in medicine which can determine the sex of a child before birth. One is called *amniocentesis*. In this test the doctor takes out a small amount of the fluid which surrounds the fetus. The fluid is then studied in a laboratory. The tests will show whether the child will have certain inherited defects.

It also tells whether the baby will be a girl or a boy, but the test isn't meant to be used for that purpose. The sex of their new baby doesn't really matter to most parents as long as it arrives healthy and normal. Besides, wondering what their baby will be is part of the fun!

Dangers to the Mother

Does the mother bleed a lot when she has a baby?

Answer: Usually not much at all—not enough to affect her normal blood count.

Do women ever die from having babies?

Answer: Occasionally a woman dies while giving birth. But if the mother has taken good care of herself, eaten the right foods, and seen her doctor regularly, the chances are good that she'll have a normal delivery.

Delivery Position

Does a baby come out headfirst or feetfirst?

Answer: Babies are usually born headfirst. However, sometimes a baby comes out feetfirst or some other way. When it's time for the baby to be born, the doctor can tell whether the child is in the best position. He can also tell whether the mother is going to be able to deliver normally. (*Deliver* is the word that's used to mean *give birth.*)

Most women have no problem. After all, God planned the whole process and made a female's uterus and vagina to stretch large enough for the baby to be born. But occasionally things don't work as well as they should.

If the doctor sees there will be a serious problem, he may decide to deliver the baby by a Caesarean or "C" section. Then the mother is taken into the surgical area of the hospital. A small cut is quickly made into her abdomen and then into her uterus. The baby is lifted out, and the uterus and abdomen are sewed shut. This operation doesn't take long, but it takes the mother a bit longer to get her strength back.

Twins and Multiple Births

What causes twins and triplets?

Answer: There are two types of twins—fraternal and identical. Some families have more than the usual number of twins, so it seems heredity plays a part. When a woman's ovary releases two or more ova or egg cells instead of the usual one, and they are fertilized, she will have more than one baby. If there are two egg cells, she will have *fraternal* twins. Each cell is entered by a separate sperm, so each has a separate placenta and is a completely different child. There may be one boy and one girl or the two may be of the same sex. Either way they're no more alike in looks than any other two kids in a family.

It's different for *identical* twins, however. When one ovum is fertilized by a single sperm, it may then split into two or more cells. If into two, it develops into two babies which have the same umbilical cord and placenta. Identical twins are always the same sex and usually look so much alike you can hardly tell them apart. They may even think alike!

Triplets and other multiple births may be either identical or fraternal. These days there seem to be more births of five or six or even more babies. One reason is that some wives who have trouble becoming pregnant may consult a doctor who may give them what's known as a fertility drug. This is a substance that can cause a woman's body to release several egg cells. Unfortunately when this happens the babies are often born too early.

Birth Defects

Why are some babies born with birth defects?

Answer: The reasons are not completely known, but there are some clues. We know, for instance, that if the mother contracts German measles while she's pregnant, there's a higher likelihood that the baby will have birth defects or will not develop properly. Other diseases and viruses may also play a part. As medical science makes new discoveries, more and more problems are being overcome.

The best thing a pregnant woman can do is to get good medical care early, to eat good food and live sensibly, to stay away from alcohol, tobacco, and medications (even over-the-counter-drugs like aspirin). Sometimes even though the mother does everything right, a child is born with problems. But the parents love the child because it's a part of them. And even though it makes them sad, they understand that God has a plan for their child too.

9. The Teen Years: Up, Up, and Away!

Older parents are fond of saying to the parents of young children: "Little children, little problems;
Big children, big problems."
Younger couples often resent this comment. Struggling to cope with rambunctious small ones, endlessly picking up after them, constantly watching out for them, these parents are understandably not convinced.

Yet in many ways this is true. Younger children do get into trouble that must be dealt with, of course. Their behavior may necessitate trips to the emergency ward for broken bones, and they probably leave a trail of debris wherever they go. Yet most of these problems are relatively minor.

With the young person in high school and college, however, the potential for serious problems is much greater. Compared to having a pregnant teenage daughter, a child's broken bone is minor. Compared to one's child's being responsible for an accident that caused someone's

87

death, a broken window is a snap. Compared to a child being hooked on drugs—or dependent on alcohol—or living with someone outside of marriage, using foul language seems hardly worth mentioning.

This is not to say the latter behaviors are right or should be condoned; it's merely to point out that the problems one may face while raising a teenager can be vastly more complex. Thus the parent whose child has entered the teenage years often feels a kind of panic. "What can I do?" the parent asks.

By the time children reach this stage of life they are involved in many activities over which a parent has little control. One simply cannot go everywhere, oversee every activity, or select friends for one's teenager. Young people want to do things on their own—and rightly so. The child must become a responsible adult. Yet the perils we parents see are very real, and our fears are understandable. What to do?

There is one essential above all others: Pray. That may sound hopelessly simplistic or like a stick-your-head-in-the-sand kind of answer, but in truth it's the only answer that carries any assurance. As Christians we can confidently turn our children over to the care and guidance of our gracious heavenly Father.

And what better answer could we have? We are limited; God is limitless. We see only what our eyes comprehend; God sees everywhere. As that familiar Bible verse puts it:

> For He shall give His angels charge over thee, to keep thee in all thy ways. They shall bear thee up in their hands, lest thou dash thy foot against a stone.
>
> Psalm 91:11-12 KJV

That verse is true for our children too!

SURPRISE! PARENTS ARE STILL ROLE MODELS

As always, our children are watching us, absorbing our values, our behavior. This is true even though they may ridicule our style of dress, the way we comb our hair, the car we drive, our life-style, even the language we use. Most children would never dream of admitting it, and probably don't realize it's true, yet we parents, by the way we live, are a major influence on their lives—now and in the future. Sooner or later most young adults begin to espouse largely the same values as their parents.

Remember Lisa, who spent most of her 13th and 14th years in her room? "The whole thing was crazy," said her mother, "but she eventually came around. By the time she was about 15½ she began to mellow. She would actually sit around the family room with the rest of us now and then. By 16 she was getting almost pleasant, and by 17 we were all on good terms again. At 18 she was telling her younger brother and sister to pay attention to us—that they didn't know how lucky they were to have us for parents. Kids! Who can figure them out?"

Teenagers also get their concept of what marriage is from us. When they see that our marriage relationship is deep and mutually enriching, when they sense husband and wife meet each other's needs, it's a clear witness that even in this world of distorted values a couple can have a satisfying marriage.

"My mom and dad were divorced when I was a small child," said Randy, "and I spent a lot of time with my best friend, Merle. I loved going to his house. That's where I first began to see what marriage could be. Merle's mom and dad were still in love—even after all those years and three kids. I couldn't believe it when we'd walk into the kitchen and they'd be hugging and kissing!

"One time I got up the nerve to ask Merle's dad why their marriage had worked, and we had a long talk. He said one thing that stood out in my mind: 'We both try to put Christ first. And we try to love each other—accept each other—as Christ would. We fail, of course, all the time. But we keep on trying. And we work at our marriage, every day, I guess if we have a secret, that's it.'

"I never forgot that conversation," said Randy. "I suppose Denise and I might have broken up long ago if I hadn't had Merle's folks to remember. They proved to me that it's possible to stay married—and stay in love."

Because of our influence on young people, it's apparent that keeping our own marriage healthy is still our No. 1 priority. For where else would we want them to get their values concerning what it means to be married? From the movies? From television? From books? Most of us would answer with an emphatic "No!" Yet those are major sources of information and influence for young people.

YOUNG PEOPLE WANT TO KNOW

Young people are curious, especially about sex. Here are questions written down and turned in by high school freshmen during a youth Bible class:
—How do you know if sex is right for you?
—How do you know if your partner cares or if you are just being used?
—How often do couples have intercourse?
—Can sperm swim through your jeans?
—How do you stop sex if you really feel you love your partner and would like to have it, but are afraid of getting pregnant?
—How does intercourse feel?
—What about birth control? How do you go about getting it?

Advantages and disadvantages of each method? What about an I.U.D.?

—What are the long-term effects of the birth control pill?

—Is it true you can't get pregnant if you have intercourse standing up?

—How safe are condoms?

—At what time of the month is a girl most likely to get pregnant? Is any time safe?

—What do you do if you find out you're pregnant?

—How does it feel to have a baby?

Surprised? These are the questions on the minds of young teenagers. Christian teenagers. And they may be the subjects most parents would rather not discuss with their young people.

"I feel uncomfortable talking about sex with our youngsters," said Ginny thoughtfully. "If we explain birth control to them, won't they think it means we're giving them permission to have intercourse? And if they *are* going all the way, I don't want to know about it! I don't think I could handle it. Besides, they've had sex education classes at school and they know all the facts—probably more than I do."

Many parents feel like Ginny. Yet when we don't talk with our teens we're out of the picture altogether. We have no chance to share our own Christian values—God's formula for living responsibly.

KNOWLEDGEABLE YOUNG PEOPLE?

The truth is that although today's young people seem sophisticated, many have faulty ideas regarding sex. Much of their information—and misinformation—comes from the media.

Consider this: An average of 27 scenes per hour on daytime and prime time programming depict, discuss, or suggest sexual behavior. In fact, Louis Harris and Associates claim that the three major television networks alone broadcast an average of 65,000 references to sexual behavior in a season. Also, consider that sexual behavior is more often shown between those who are *not* married to each other. If we multiply those figures by the number of years our child has been watching TV, we'll begin to understand why surveys show the majority of today's young people, ages 13 to 18, see nothing wrong with premarital sex.

THE CHILLING STATISTICS

Those attitudes are reflected in the rising rates of sexually-transmitted disease (STD). Ponder these facts:
—STD is rampant in the U.S., Canada, and other Western countries, especially among the young.
—Gonorrhea is spreading at the fastest rate among young teenagers.
—It's estimated that every year from 60,000 to 100,000 young American women are made sterile by gonorrhea or chlamydia, unaware that they have the disease. (Statistics for Canada and other Western countries are similarly alarming.)

But there's additional evidence that times are changing—and not necessarily for the better:
—Most sexual intercourse between teenage boys and girls takes place in the home of one or the other while the parents are away.
—Each year more than one million teenage girls in the U.S. become pregnant. Four out of five are unmarried; 30,000 are under the age of 15.
—More than 500,000 pregnant American teenagers will carry their babies to term, and about 125,000 of these are under age 15.
—The teenage abortion rate is rising rapidly (an estimated 450,000 yearly), comprising about one-third of all abortions.
—Of every 100 unwed American teenage mothers, 97 choose to keep their infants, usually with little social stigma attached.
—Some sources estimate that three out of four brides under age 20 are pregnant on their wedding day.

These statistics are not meant to frighten—only to point out the necessity for strong Christian moral values in our young people. And to remind us how important it is for us to speak of our faith (and live it) with our own teenagers.

SCARE TACTICS ARE NOT THE ANSWER

Statistics are not likely to impress our children. Surprising though it seems in this scientific age, young people—especially girls—still cling to the idea that "It couldn't happen to me." And although birth control methods have proliferated and are much more available, most teens pass them up. Sometimes it's because they don't really understand, but often they feel it's more "romantic" when sexual intercourse is unplanned.

Some psychologists believe that many young unwed mothers become pregnant on purpose.

Listen to Andrea, a mother at age 16: "I guess I really wanted to get p.g. I wanted to show everyone—especially my folks—that I was grown-up and they couldn't tell me what to do. You know? They don't care about me, anyhow. No one does. But a baby of my own . . . well, my baby would always love me, I thought, no matter what. And no one could ever take it away from me. Besides, school was a drag!

"So I had my baby, a little girl. My folks had kicked me out, so I went on welfare and it's been rough. Sometimes when I've been up half the night with Alison and I'm dead on my feet, I think I must have been crazy to get into this mess. If school was a drag, having a kid is 100 times worse! . . . And the father? Oh, you mean Jay. When he heard I was p.g. and wouldn't get an abortion, he split. He didn't love me—nobody does! But I have a new boyfriend now. . . He says *he* really cares. . . ."

Unfortunately, Andrea will probably be "p.g." again before very long—and alone—and searching for "love." We live in a world where such actions are not only tolerated but expected—where young people are often under considerable pressure to "get with it."

STRENGTH FOR LIVING IN TODAY'S SOCIETY

Christian young people, too, live in this world. They feel the same emotions, struggle with the same temptations as their peers. Although we may wish it were so, our children don't go through life encased in a protective bubble. But we parents can help them learn to be strong.

How? By being open and accepting in our conversations with them. By talking of how Christ's teachings relate to our lives with others. Jesus said:

> "Love the Lord your God with all your heart, with all your soul, and with all your mind." This is the greatest and the most important commandment. The second most important commandment is like it: "Love your neighbor as you love yourself."
>
> Matthew 22:37-39 TEV

These are Christ's fundamentals for any kind of relationship. Sexual permissiveness, with its great potential for causing emotional and physical harm, contradicts these principles. Using people, achieving our own emotional gratification at the expense of another, hurting another human being, are all things we would not want done to us, all evidence of selfishness. And selfishness is now—as it always was—sin.

Christ knew, of course, that the rest of the world would behave differently and attempt to influence us. The Bible has the key to dealing with that pressure too.

Do not conform yourselves to the standards of this world, but let God transform you inwardly by a complete change of your mind.

Romans 12:2 TEV

To live as Christ's persons, to be strong enough to be different, does not come from our own efforts. Rather we allow God to make us strong—from the inside out!

IT'S NEVER EASY

Even so, living the Christian life is never easy. Changing attitudes make it much more difficult, especially for teens. "I'd hate to be young these days," said Lois, frowning. "It's got to be much harder. Lots of us toed the mark only because we were scared silly. The neighbors were always peeking out their windows, and the older people in our town and our church kept an eye on us. And we knew it! Aunts, uncles, and cousins all made it their business to lecture us if they thought we had it coming. As for contraception, such products were hard to get—if we'd even known what to do with them. And if a girl got pregnant, well, her whole family was disgraced.

"Now families are scattered, and I'm not sure they'd speak up, anyhow. In fact, I don't know if *I* would. . . . I guess we all have the attitude that 'It's not *my* problem.' Today a young person can easily buy birth control products—probably from a clerk who doesn't even look surprised. And unwed teenage mothers are bringing their babies to school with them. Seems to me a teenager nowadays has to be good just because he or she wants to—because they sure don't get much help!"

Lois is right. But in spite of today's permissiveness, there is still a large segment among teens who do *not* choose to engage in sexual activity. Unfortunately, parents often assume otherwise. This can give a young person a feeling of "What's the use? I'm pronounced guilty no matter what I do!" The result is usually an atmosphere of resentment and alienation.

THOSE INEVITABLE CONFLICTS

Sometimes, in spite of our best efforts, a situation arises where our children feel we don't trust them. We may refuse permission to go on a weekend trip with a group of new friends, for instance.

"The way we handle such things," says Jane, "is to tell our daughter, 'Look, we trust you as a person. But we don't feel you have the maturity and experience yet to make all of your own decisions. You could end up in a situation you're not equipped to handle. So we have to say no.' Our daughter seems able to accept that explanation without too much hassle because it doesn't attack her personally."

94

As parents we have a right to say, "Our family rule is . . ." Young people want to know the acceptable limits, even when they protest. In fact it's often a relief when they can say, "My folks want me in by midnight."

Should our children occasionally come home later than the agreed-upon time, we'll accept their reasonable excuse. After all, young people do have car trouble at times. They do go to concerts and movies which run later than they expect. They do become deeply engrossed in talking with a friend and lose track of time. (Haven't we done the same at times with our own good friends?)

When we know our young people to be generally reliable, we can show our trust, even when circumstances seem contrary. If we believe the subject demands discussion, a good way to begin is by saying, "Perhaps you think I won't understand, but I promise I'll try. Could we talk about it?"

It is, of course, a different situation if we've had problems with our child lying to us. In general, we'll do well to "put the best construction on everything." For if we show that we believe our children and emphasize the importance of being trustworthy, more often than not they'll try to live up to our expectations.

THE BEST KIND OF PARENTAL LOVE

As Christian parents we'll avoid needless confrontations except when our teens are acting in a manner clearly contrary to God's will.

"My folks were really great, all those years when I was a teenager and giving them a hard time," says Erica. "Deep down I knew they loved me, no matter what, and that they were proud of me as a person, even when they didn't like what I had done. Sure, I disappointed them sometimes—and they me—but we were a family and our love went on. I can't tell you what that meant to me, when everything else in my life often seemed upside down."

Our teens need our respect, as well, if they're to respect themselves and others. For instance, we'd never say to one of our own friends (especially in front of contemporaries), "John, are you ever going to get that hair cut? Must you always look like a shaggy dog?" Nor would we appreciate it if we were in a gathering with friends and someone said to us, "Are you sure you want to have dessert? You can barely get your pants buttoned as it is!" Neither would we call to an adult departing with a date, "Now remember what I told you. Act like a lady and behave yourself!"

Yet some parents are prone to issue similar reminders in ringing tones, regardless of how many people are present. Such insensitivity can immeasurably damage a child's self-esteem.

All this may seem far removed from sexuality. But when we respect our young people, their own feelings of self-worth are strengthened. And a healthy self-image is necessary to develop into an adult able to relate well on all levels, including sex.

COMMUNICATION IS IMPORTANT

The attitude we want to cultivate with our young people is that they can tell us anything at any time. However, we should be ready to really listen. "I remember trying to talk to my dad," says Jordan. "But he never heard what I said. I could sense he was just waiting for me to pause so he could jump in and tell me what I was doing wrong. He always had the 'perfect solution' all ready to lay out for me.

"What *I* thought, what *I* felt, didn't really matter. He didn't care. He was more concerned with giving answers than with hearing questions. After awhile I just avoided talking with him because we had no real communication."

Jordan makes a good point. Communication is meant to be two persons talking—and listening. "I never really knew how to listen until I read a book on effective communication," said Sally. "Now I try to follow those guidelines. I listen to the kids and then repeat what I think they've said before answering. They do the same. At first it seemed awkward to all of us, but now it's a habit. It's super! At last we really *hear* each other!"

Another part of true communication is hearing what's *behind* the words. When we talk with our teenagers, for instance, we'll want to know what they're feeling, not just surface details. For we can only reach understanding when we perceive what's inside.

96

Open communication doesn't require that our young people tell us every last detail of every thought, word, and deed. For example, most of the time teenagers won't get too explicit about the details of their dates, nor should we attempt to pry. But once they've confided in us, if we then use that information to scold or threaten or make cutting remarks, they'll not share secret thoughts with us again. And who can blame them?

When we talk with our child about sexuality, we'll want to verbalize and communicate our feelings, as well. If we're uncomfortable, maybe we're emulating our own parents' attitudes with us. Those old patterns die hard. Even parents who feel very emancipated may find themselves hesitant about discussing sex with an aware teenager.

CHANGING PATTERNS

In the past it was assumed that every young male wanted to progress from kissing to touching to intercourse. Girls were considered more inhibited and likely to be coerced into sexual activity by their boyfriends. Today many teenage girls and young women are quite aggressive and may openly approach a young man.

"I took Heather to a movie the other night and boy! did she come on strong," says Darren. "She kept leaning against me in the theater, and after the show she told me her folks were gone for the weekend, so why didn't we go to her place and have sex? She said she's on the pill, so why worry?

"I didn't know what to do—I hardly knew her! So I told her I had to get the car home so my sister could go to work, and I beat it. Most of the guys I know would give their right arm for a chance with Heather. Is there something wrong with me?"

Young people of both sexes need reassurance they're not "undersexed" or abnormal in any way when they choose not to become sexually active. Rather they're to be commended for their wisdom and maturity, for sticking to their own values in spite of pressure.

Today both the young male and the young female may see intercourse as conquest, proof that they're worldly wise and attractive. Both may matter-of-factly expect to get or give sexual favors in reward for a big date. After all, they've seen it on television and in the movies: date, come home, and end up in bed. It's a standard procedure!

So each has a responsibility for setting the tone for their relationship in the beginning, quietly and kindly. Even so, the old arguments will likely be used:

—"But I can't stand it! Do you want me to get sick? Or go crazy or something?"

—"It's just not natural to deny ourselves when we both care about each other."

97

—"Of course I don't just want your body! I care about you as a person."

—"How can we have a meaningful relationship without sex?"

—"Sure, I'll always respect you, no matter what."

—Etc., etc., etc.

The logic is as faulty as it ever was. With the added pressure of today's permissive society, young people need to carefully think through their own values—form their own solid foundation. It's helpful, too, when youngsters understand not only their own bodies but those of the other sex.

(Book Five of the Learning about Sex series, *Love, Sex, and God,* by Bill Ameiss and Jane Graver, is written just for teenagers. It not only explains bodily functions and self-image, but also explores boy-girl relationships from the Christian perspective.)

WHY DO WE HOLD OUR PERSONAL VALUES?

Before we discuss values with our young people, we must do some personal soul-searching. What do we believe? Why? Have we thought it through in light of today or are we just parroting words and slogans? If it's the latter, be assured our youngster will see right through it and discount what we say. Especially if we begin, "When I was your age, young people wouldn't dream of . . ."

But talk we must. There are many subjects to discuss, and it helps to remember:

—Casual sex can never be what God intended the sexual relationship to be. People who consider sex as a fleeting encounter or "just good fun" usually have never known anything deeper.

—There's no medical or psychological evidence that postponing sexual intercourse causes any lasting physical or emotional harm to male or female.

—When sexual intercourse is expected as payment for a date, it's like cheap prostitution.

—The dangers of VD are very real. The person infected with VD is often unaware of it; therefore the more sexual contacts, the greater the risk.

—There is no absolutely safe period when a female can be assured of not becoming pregnant.

—Other than abstinence there is no 100% foolproof method of birth control, even when directions are followed correctly.

—Even when the male withdraws his penis before ejaculation, there may be early leakage of sperm before withdrawal. Pregnancy can result.

—Teenage mothers are twice as likely to die from hemorrhage and/or miscarriage.

—Babies born to teenage mothers are two to three times as likely to die during the first year of life.

—Teenage mothers often spend their lives on welfare. A large portion of the federal Aid to Families with Dependent Children budget goes to households where the mother gave birth in her teens.

—Women who become mothers in their teen years are likely to have jobs with less status, lower incomes, and less satisfaction all through their lives.

—People who become parents during their teens may be more likely to become child abusers because of resentment over what they've missed.

—80% of teen-age marriages end in divorce within five years.

BETTER TOO SOON THAN TOO LATE!

It's important to talk with our children early, before the young person closes up like a clam. By the time young people are dating (or their friends are) their perspective will have changed, their opinions formed. Then our effort to communicate Christian values may seem like a contrary, personal judgment of them or their peers.

We start by being frank, by communicating our love and acceptance. Perhaps we might begin by saying: "I'll answer any questions you want to throw at me. If I don't know the answers I'll find them. I'll listen to your opinions and try to understand what you believe and why. I hope you'll do the same for me. . . .

"Sometimes young people think they 'owe' each other sex. Some may think having intercourse will prove they're liberated. But liberation means being *free*, not giving in to someone else's standards. Neither your best friend nor the crowd nor the person you date—nor society—should dictate what *you* do. And because you're a Christian that's especially true."

"LOVE" ISN'T ALWAYS LOVE

"You see, many times what seems like 'love' is simply sexual attraction—something you could feel with many different people at various periods of your life. But to love someone—to enter into a sexual *relationship* (and as Christians we believe that must be as a married couple)—involves much more: commitment for life, faithfulness, respecting the other's right to be an individual, willingness to put the other person before oneself, the desire to build a life together. It means 'we' is more important than 'I.'

"And contrary to what most people think, love is not just an emotion; it's a daily decision! Most people aren't ready for that until they've had time to find out who they are themselves and what they

99

want to do with their lives—until they've developed the ability to see themselves and each other clearly and logically, accepting each other as they are.

"It also means being ready to take total responsibility for one's own life and actions, as well as the responsibility of a child, because that's always a possibility. It means being ready to put aside one's own goals, if necessary, for the good of the family.

"If you enter a sexual relationship outside of marriage, you may be letting yourself in for a lot of pain—and cause pain for others, too. Part of that pain is sneaking around. Think about God's plan for us: a husband and wife committed to life together, secure in each other's love, with time to grow together and work out any problems. God's plan works so well, in fact, that anything else is second-best!"

This can also be a good time to discuss again some of the material from the previous chapter, which deals with the sexual relationship in more detail. Of course, we'll not deliver all this information nonstop. Nor can we now sit back and say, "Well, that takes care of that!" Our young people are constantly changing and will have new concerns, new questions, at various times along the way to maturity. That's why communication is best when it's easy and open—and ongoing.

BACKING UP WORDS WITH ACTION

Young people demonstrate growing maturity by their behavior and by adopting a sound set of values. We parents play a major part in establishing those values. All through the growing-up years we try to live by the principles we proclaim. Now that's even more vital, for nothing more easily makes a young person cynical about adult integrity than a do-as-I-say-not-as-I-do attitude.

"My dad's always lecturing me about honesty," said 17-year-old Jason, "and I used to be proud of him because I thought he was different. Lately I've been finding out he's not. Like when he was bragging about what he got away with on the income tax return. Or when the restaurant cashier gave him change for a 20-dollar bill and he'd only given her a 10. Next time he gives me that old honesty routine, I'm gonna tell him what I really think!"

Parents give other kinds of conflicting messages, too. For instance, we may say we want our youngsters to avoid emotional entanglements. Yet we may actually push them into early dating and/or sexual activity (usually without realizing it). As an example, our daughter may not be as popular as we'd like, so we pressure her to date—anyone. Or we may be vaguely fearful a child could have homosexual tendencies and view dating as "proof" to the contrary. Sometimes we get personal satisfaction from knowing our youngster is much sought after.

If we want our young people to heed our counsel, they need assurance that we live what we say.

UNFLATTERING COMPARISONS

Today's youngsters appear to be brighter, more talented and attractive, more in control. Indeed, parents may even feel uncomfortable around their teenagers. Father may become newly conscious that his largest measurement is now around his middle instead of his manly chest. He stands next to his handsome son, who towers above him, and is acutely conscious of thinning hair and sagging jowls.

For her part, Mother sees her daughter in bikini or short shorts, notes the fresh, unwrinkled face and sparkling eyes, and sighs. Did she ever look that stunning? Suddenly both parents feel old and dumpy, a bit self-conscious around their own children and their friends.

But it's quite possible for parents to be friends with their children, without in any way being in competition. It means that we esteem ourselves as we are—and our children as individuals in their own right. It's important frequently to reaffirm our love, too. An arm around the shoulders, a pat on the back—just simple human contact— is all it takes. The youngster may react by seeming uncomfortable or impatient, but that simply reflects the process of growing away from the parent-child relationship.

Our acceptance and affection, the way we relate to our young people now, will have a lasting effect. The satisfying true friendships we desire with our grown children have their roots in these teen years.

HANDLING THE UNTHINKABLE

Suppose, however, that we've tried to do everything right, but it all seems to go wrong. What approach should we take?

The same reaction that our gracious God has when *we* sin: forgiving love. Love gives us no alternative. For if we take a you-made-your-bed-now-lie-in-it attitude, what will we accomplish? This young person needs our emotional support and our tender acceptance, even though we in no way approve what has happened.

For we, too, have made—and will make—mistakes. It is sin, yes, but Jesus Christ died for the redemption of sin. *All* sin. Can we do less than to stand by our children through such a time and try to help them find direction? True, there is pain for everyone involved. But we—and our young people—may well grow through pain.

THE KEY TO SURVIVING PARENTHOOD

As Christians, struggling to be understanding, patient parents of teenagers, we'll display trust in our children; work to strengthen our relationship; frequently reinforce their self-esteem and sense of identity; talk openly—and listen. We'll daily commit our young people to God's loving care and ask His forgiveness for their mistakes and our own. And we'll take courage from the words of 1 Peter 4:8:

> Above everything else be sure that you have real deep love for one another, remembering how love can "cover a multitude of sins" (Phillips).

QUESTIONS PARENTS ASK

Dating Age

What's the right age for dating?

Answer: There is no "right" age. It depends on an individual family's standards and the maturity of the young people involved. It's generally considered advisable for young teens to get to know a large number of people so they can choose dating partners more wisely.

Friendships

Can teenage males and females really be "just friends"?

Answer: Today's teens seem able to have real friendships with those of the other sex without any romantic entanglement. Perhaps they've learned to consider people as individuals, and look for qualities that would make for good friends, disregarding gender.

Teens Entertaining When Parents Are Gone

My husband travels a lot in his work, and he often asks me to go along. I enjoy it, and our children are teenagers now, well able to care for themselves. But I don't feel right leaving them alone. I'm afraid they'll give a wild party or something. Am I being silly?

Answer: Many parents as a general principle forbid their children to entertain anyone in the home when they're not present. Since researchers now tell us that most sexual activity between teenagers occurs in the home while the parents are gone, it seems prudent to avoid providing opportunities for temptation. (One alternative would be to limit guests to a specified number of the same sex as your child.)

One way to approach this subject without insulting the teenager's sense of trustworthiness and maturity is to say something like this: "Of course we trust you. We trust your integrity and your values and your good intentions. But we don't think you've had enough experience just yet for us to trust your judgment. We feel the same way about your friends. That's the reason for our family policy that you don't have anyone in the house when we're not here.

"You probably don't agree, but we love you and care about what could happen to you more than anything, so this is the way our family will operate."

This policy could be reviewed as your teenagers get older and show more maturity. But even then you'll probably want to lay down some conditions. You may also wish to emphasize that you don't want your youngsters going to a friend's home when his or her parents aren't around. However, this is much more difficult to enforce.

Foul Language

My teenager has a foul mouth! When I scold, his reply is, "Don't be so square! All my friends talk this way." Is that true?

Answer: Children and teenagers often feel they automatically become more grown-up if they use such language. Or they may simply be reflecting the language they hear at school; perhaps the "in" crowd talks this way. On the other hand, some children delight in using such language and/or in telling dirty jokes precisely because they know they'll get a shocked reaction from adults.

As Christians, of course, we're to be different from the world, and the Bible gives us many guidelines:

Keep thy tongue from evil, and thy lips from speaking guile.
Psalm 34:13 KJV
Set a watch, O Lord, before my mouth; keep the door of my lips.
Psalm 141:3 KJV

Rather than shame our child or try to manipulate behavior through conveying guilt, we Christian parents can quietly state: "This is what the Bible teaches, and this is our standard as a Christian family. Therefore please don't use that kind of language in our home." You can't control what your child says when away from you, of course, but you have a right to establish firm principles within your home.

In addition, you can point out that many people are offended by such language. And since people are often judged by the way they talk, your child may miss out on some friendships or opportunities if speech standards are low.

If your child seems to have a need to use obscenities constantly, try to find time for a long talk. Are there deep problems which trouble him? Is the youngster feeling isolated or rejected, either from his peers or his family? Does this young person have a low self-image, a need to continually "prove" unworthiness by flouting society and family standards?

If, after such a discussion, your youngster still seems to have a compulsion to use foul language, it may be the sign of deeply rooted problems and you may wish to seek professional counseling.

Pornography

I found some dirty pictures in my son's room. How should I have handled it?

Answer: At some time in their growing-up years most boys possess some pornographic and/or erotic materials, which are increasingly easy to obtain. Often youngsters think this gives them a pictorial illustration of "what it's all about." After all, they reason, how else will they know what to do when their time comes? There are women's magazines with male centerfolds, and there is pornography produced for females, so young girls may also acquire such material.

The human body is not "dirty." Some of the greatest, most enduring works of art portray the nude human form. Christians see the human body as a marvel of God's creation—which it is! Pornography, however, is meant to be shocking, meant to be lewd. Pornography is a distortion of what God intends for the body.

Should you discover pornographic material belonging to your child, resist the impulse to launch into a lecture. Your loud, intense pronouncements will only make this forbidden fruit sweeter. Rather, recognize that sexual curiosity is natural.

But you may want to have a low-key discussion. Look at the pornography together. Human beings are almost always portrayed in a dehumanizing manner. Typically a female is shown as an object, being used by a male for his own sexual gratification. Or the poses are deliberately intended to arouse the viewer sexually. In other words, pornography reduces sexuality to a function, the human body to a thing, and does away completely with the idea of a caring and committed relationship between man and woman. This destroys God's concept of personhood. And we all want to be appreciated for the person we are, not just as gratification machines.

The greatest danger of heavy pornography viewing is that these attitudes may be absorbed by impressionable young people. They may not yet have the insight to realize that a sexual relationship involves more—much more—than two sets of sex organs. In most cases an open, frank discussion with an understanding parent will tarnish the glitter of such material. Most young people are extremely idealistic. Once they recognize the dehumanizing character of such trash, it will likely lose most of its appeal.

Explaining Sexual Intercourse to Teens

I told my youngsters the "facts of life" long ago. Can't I assume they understand all about sexual intercourse?

Answer: No, because they are older now and will comprehend differently. They're also more personally interested in the subject. You may wish to say something like this:

"God gave males and females a very special marriage gift called sexual intercourse. Husbands and wives love each other very much—so much that there are times when they want to be close and caress

each other and touch each other all over. They want to show how much they love and care for each other, and words just don't seem to be enough. At those times a couple may want to have sexual intercourse.

"When the husband thinks how much he loves his wife and wants to be really, really close, his thoughts send an impulse to his nerves and arteries. This causes the spongy tissue of the penis to fill with blood and to become hard and straight, in preparation for intercourse.

"The wife's desire for her husband causes her body to get ready, too. Her vagina gets softer and more relaxed and begins secreting a lubricating substance. This will make intercourse more comfortable for both partners.

"The husband places his penis into his wife's vagina. Their bodies fit together just the way God designed! The couple enjoys the way their closeness feels, because it's something special, just for the two of them.

"As the husband and wife begin to move their bodies together in harmony, each feels very pleasurable sensations. A sense of excitement grows and grows, and may reach its peak in what's known as orgasm or climax. During orgasm the husband ejaculates. That means that sperm forcefully move from his penis into the wife's vagina. This is accompanied by good feelings for the man and does not cause his wife any discomfort. In case you're wondering, sperm and urine never pass at the same time.

"The wife doesn't ejaculate, of course, but she may also reach orgasm. Her emotions are just as intense, just as pleasing as the husband's.

"After ejaculation the male's penis begins to return to its original state, which is soft and limp. Both marriage partners are filled with a feeling of total relaxation, warmth, and love for each other. That may be where the term 'making love' came from, because sexual intercourse between marriage partners does make their feeling of love for each other seem new all over again. They remember all the other times like this, all the years they've shared a life together—the good times and the not-so-good times—and they feel very, very close to each other.

"Of course, it's possible for a male and female to have sexual intercourse without any love at all. It can be just two bodies coming together. But that's not what God had in mind when He made us.

"One of the best things about a couple's sexual relationship is that no matter how many years they're married, they can still want each other sexually. They can still find great joy and satisfaction in their sexual relationship. Sexual intercourse between husband and wife is one of God's best gifts to human beings.

"It may take a couple some time to make their sexual relationship work as it should. Even when the bride and groom love each other very much, it sometimes takes awhile until they become tuned-in to each other, until sexual intercourse is completely enjoyable for both of them."

106

Explaining Orgasm

Help! My teenager wants to know what an orgasm or climax feels like. How do I explain it?

Answer: Depending on the age of your young person, you may wish to say something like this: "There's nothing I could say that would really tell you how an orgasm feels, because it's different for each person. One doctor says it's like a sneeze, and that's probably as good a comparison as any.

"You know how you feel when you have a sneeze coming on? How your whole body seems to be concentrating on the sneeze and you can't even think of anything else? And then after you've finally sneezed, you feel relaxed and peaceful? That's a bit what orgasm is like. During sexual intercourse a person's whole body is tensed up in anticipation, and then there's a sort of explosive feeling, just as a sneeze is an explosion in your nose. And then you feel warm and good and relaxed and peaceful all over."

Talking to Teens About Responsible Sexuality

My teenager seems so sophisticated that I feel awkward talking about the dangers of premarital intercourse. What can I say?

Answer: Young people often try to appear knowledgeable about sex, especially around their parents. For one thing, they may feel self-conscious. For another, they may be sure they'll be in for a long lecture, perhaps packed with parental emotion. So the first rule is: Try not to preach. Allow the youngster to express opinions, and don't betray surprise or shock or make judgments. For if you do, your child will neither hear what you say nor respond.

You've probably already discussed sexual intercourse and the basic facts covered in Chapter 8. You may want to briefly discuss them again and then take it one step further. A key concept which young people will usually accept is that of personal responsibility. There's a lot of ground to cover, and you may wish to say any of the following which may fit a given occasion:

"Maybe you've begun to feel something special about one person in particular. When you begin to care about someone, you just naturally want to be close—to touch and hold that person. And when these feelings become very strong you may very much want to have sexual intercourse with that person. God put that desire into us; He made us sexual beings. And He invented marriage as the special relationship in which a husband and wife are to have sexual intercourse.

"Having intercourse with someone outside of marriage is a sin against God and the other person. No matter how someone may try to make it look right, intercourse outside of marriage comes down to people putting their own pleasure first—before obedience to God or before the deeper relationship of love that God intended marriage to be.

"In marriage a man and a woman promise to love each other, to care for each other, and to be faithful to each other—for life. Then they establish a home of their own—a life of their own—and they're proud of it. They don't have to make excuses to anyone. Best of all, they have plenty of time to learn how to have a good, satisfying sexual relationship.

"You see, it's more than a couple getting into bed together and WHAM! it's dynamite!—the way it happens in the movies. Even for most married couples it takes time—for some a few weeks, for some several months. And for some it may take a year or more.

"The point is: Married couples know they have time to work it out. They know their partner isn't going to walk out and find someone else just because their sexual adjustment is taking awhile. They've committed their lives to each other, so they have the freedom to be themselves.

"Their commitment also means they're ready to be responsible for whatever comes—to care for each other when sick, to support each other emotionally and financially—and to take the responsibility of a child if the wife becomes pregnant.

"Ever since you had your first menstrual period (wet dream) you've been physically capable of becoming a mother (father). Maybe the idea of having a baby of your own sounds exciting to you—or maybe it sounds ridiculous. In any case, it's always a real possibility for a couple having intercourse—even when they practice birth control.

"You've probably heard about some of the different kinds of birth control. Some of them are the condom (rubber), which fits over the penis; the diaphragm, which fits over the mouth of the uterus and must be fitted by a medical professional; various kinds of vaginal tablets, foams, and creams. There is also the birth control pill, which a woman must get by prescription and must take daily. She must be examined regularly by a doctor, too, because the pill can have harmful side effects.

"In 'natural family planning' methods (the only methods recognized by the Roman Catholic Church) a woman closely keeps track of her monthly periods, avoiding intercourse during those times each month when she is most likely to get pregnant.

"Sometimes young people think that if they use birth control they can have sex at any time. 'After all,' they may say, 'why not? We're not hurting anyone, and there won't be a baby.' So they may have intercourse first with one person, then with another, and they think this means they're free, liberated—grown up.

"But there's *no* way to avoid the chance of pregnancy except to avoid having intercourse. Nothing else is 100% foolproof. Not even the pill. Not even if the male withdraws his penis before ejaculation, because there's often an early leakage of small amounts of sperm long before he ejaculates.

"So for all practical purposes, every time a couple has intercourse they should be ready to assume full responsibility for a child. Most young people are far from ready for that. Even if they really love each other and decide to get married because they're going to have a baby, it's not easy. Too many things make it tough.

"The young husband usually has to quit school to take a low-paying job and may never finish his education, so he's stuck with less income all his life. The young wife is twice as likely to die from the complications of pregnancy. Her baby is two or three times as apt to die during its first year than if she were an adult. Their marriage is much more likely to end in divorce, too, than if the same two people had married in their 20s, when they were more mature.

"Perhaps you're thinking the girl could always get an abortion. It's true that abortions are much more available than they used to be. Sometimes you hear people say that having an abortion is just a simple little procedure, that it's all over in a few minutes and all your problems are behind you. But it's not that easy.

"For one thing, an unborn baby is more than just 'a problem' or an inconvenience. It's a real human being (Psalm 139). Killing it is killing a human being. Also, a girl who has an abortion, even when she seems calm and levelheaded and quite casual about the whole thing, often develops emotional problems that cause a lot of problems in the future—maybe even affect her ability to relate to her husband later on. Once she's had an abortion, a girl may have trouble with future pregnancies, too, when she and her husband may want a child very much.

"Another factor to recognize is the prevalence of VD, especially among young people. Many of the drugs that were hailed as miracle cures a few years back don't do the job anymore because the bacteria have developed a resistance to them. Besides, several of the venereal diseases give no sign at all that one is infected. So a young man or woman may be infecting everyone with whom he or she has intercourse and never even know it. Worst of all, VD can cause permanent damage, so that when people marry and want to have children they may find that VD has made them sterile.

"So you see, these sexual feelings you're having now have many implications. It's not nearly so simple as it sounds. When people talk about the sex drive and how we must satisfy it, they aren't considering the whole person and the emotions involved. Sometimes it almost seems as if they think people are just sex organs with a body attached!

"But God gave us a conscience, a brain, and emotions as well—love and caring and self-control. 'Self-control' sounds almost out-of-date, but it's still valid. Self-control does no damage to either male or female. But giving in to our sexual urges outside of marriage does, because it's sin. A better term for you and me as Christians would be 'God-control,' for He has promised that we can lean on His strength no matter what the temptation.

"Now that you're becoming an adult, more and more you are making your own decisions. Sometimes that can be difficult, but you're not in this alone. Christ died to free you—and me—from being slaves to feelings that are wrong."

> You *belong* to the power which you choose to obey, whether you choose sin, whose reward is death, or God, obedience to whom means the reward of righteousness.
>
> Romans 6:16 Phillips

"Lots of young people—and grownups too—think that sex outside of marriage is sophisticated. But being 'with it' isn't half so worthwhile or satisfying as being strong in Christ. Because when we choose to follow His teachings, we have inner peace. And that's one of the best things in life."

Note to Parents

It's easy to make this sound like a sermon. That's almost guaranteed to make your young person tune you out! Strive to make this a dialog;

along the way ask what your teenager thinks about what you're saying. If there's disagreement at times (and there probably will be), don't judge or scold. Talk about both viewpoints and try to be objective.

Most of all, point to the Scriptures and to Christ, the authority Christians accept also in matters of sexual values. Note how, for example, in 1 Corinthians 6:13 ff., St. Paul urges God's love for us in Christ as the reason and the power for Christians not only to abstain from immorality but to grow in fulfilling their God-intended sexuality. In searching Scriptures like these together, be warm and caring; communicate that you *know* your youngster's feelings because you've struggled with them, too. Emphasize that sexual feelings aren't in themselves wrong. Rather, as good gifts of God, they're a potent force which should be wisely used at appropriate times in a person's life—to God's glory.

> Do you not know that your body is a temple of the Holy Spirit within you, which you have from God? You are not your own; you were bought with a price. So glorify God in your body.
>
> 1 Corinthians 6:19-20 RSV

Should Parents Give Teenagers the Pill?

My friend is giving her teenage daughter the birth control pill. She says she knows the girl will be having intercourse anyway and it would be terrible if she got pregnant. She maintains that all parents should face reality and do the same, because it's the lesser of two evils. Is she right?

Answer: This may be a fairly common practice today, but your friend's logic is faulty. It's *not* inevitable that teens will be sexually active; many choose not to be. When a parent gives a child any kind of birth control device, several things happen—all negative:

* The parent is, in effect, saying, "Of course you will be sexually active" and thus implies approval.
* There is no principle of values or of sexual restraint to which the teenager can aspire.
* For the teens who want to avoid sexual activity, this adds one more pressure. Not only the world and their peers but also their parents are "pushing" early sex. They may well decide, "What's the use of fighting it?"

* Once sexual activity has begun, there is an ongoing temptation to become careless in using contraception.

Remember, too, that the pill provides no protection against venereal disease.

111

Teenage sexual activity is a fact of life, and of course young people should have thorough sex education and a knowledge of birth control. As parents we should counsel with our teens, keep the lines of communication open, and try to instill the desire to live a Christian life. That includes giving them our matter-of-fact expectation—our trust—that they'll live by our family standards—and God's. Surely that is a more positive approach than handing out birth control products.

The "Pap" Test

When should girls start having them? How often?

Answer: This is a laboratory test to determine whether there are any abnormal cells, which could signal the possibility of early malignancy. In doing this test the doctor uses a long cotton swab to take a small specimen of fluid from the cervix (the mouth of the uterus).

Because this test is valuable in spotting cancer in its beginning stages (when it can be much more easily cured), most doctors recommend that every woman, beginning in her late teens, have a regular "Pap" smear. The doctor will advise how often to repeat the test. If a woman is taking the birth control pill or is on hormone therapy, most physicians insist on regular vaginal examinations and more frequent "Pap" tests.

Sexually-Transmitted Disease/Venereal Disease

I hear a lot of talk about STD—is that the same as VD? How much shall I tell my child? I'm confused myself!

Answer: STD is the current and more precise term for what was formerly called VD. Both refer to diseases that are sexually transmitted. The list is long, but we all need to know the facts And it's important to help our children understand, so they have truth rather than rumor. Here, in alphabetical order, is a rundown on STD.

AIDS (*Acquired Immune Deficiency Syndrome*)

When the Centers for Disease Control in Atlanta, Georgia, issued a report on five young homosexual men in Los Angeles who had contracted an unusual form of pneumonia (*Pneumocystis carinii*), no one imagined it was the beginning of an epidemic. Nor did anyone guess that this new disease complex would be lethal. That was June 5, 1981.

By early 1988 it was estimated that 1.5 million U.S. citizens were infected with the AIDS virus, human immunodeficiency virus (HIV). Most are capable of transmitting the disease to others, although they may be unaware that they've been exposed and may appear perfectly healthy. Typically, those persons who have been exposed to the AIDS virus and

112

who possess antibodies follow a similar pattern. Within five years, 20% will develop full-fledged AIDS, 30% will develop ARC (AIDS Related Complex), and 50% will show no symptoms at all, but could transmit the HIV. Two years following diagnosis, 70% of the patients will have died. At three years, about 85% of AIDS patients will have died.

No one is ever known to have recovered normal immune function after having lost it to the AIDS virus. And drawing on test results from frozen blood samples, along with medical records, scientists now believe that it *can* take up to 10 years between exposure and development of the AIDS disease.

What's the difference between AIDS and ARC?

Answer: Both are caused by the HIV, although ARC is often less severe than classic AIDS. Both are diagnosed by a blood test, and although related, each has its own specific set of clinical symptoms. Symptoms of ARC may include appetite loss, unexplained weight loss, fever, night sweats, diarrhea, tiredness, skin rashes, lack of resistance to infection, and/or swollen lymph nodes. ARC may or may not develop into the more severe AIDS.

Symptoms of AIDS may include persistent cough and fever associated with shortness of breath or difficulty in breathing. These may be symptoms of *Pneumocystis carinii* pneumonia. Multiple bumps and purplish blotches on the skin may signal Kaposi's sarcoma, a type of cancer.

(Note: Since other conditions may cause similar symptoms to those listed, *do not* attempt to diagnose yourself. Leave that task to a qualified health professional.)

Why don't they just vaccinate people against AIDS?

Answer: Development of a vaccine—or a cure—is made more difficult because the HIV is an evolving virus—it is forever changing its makeup. There is presently no cure and no vaccine for AIDS. Dozens of drugs are being tested in human trials, and some are already approved. Zidovidine (formerly known as AZT) has been the first drug to win Food and Drug Administration (FDA) approval. But it's extremely expensive and can only prolong life; AZT does not cure AIDS.

You mean that AIDS always kills? How can that be?

Answer: The HIV virus invades the bloodstream and attacks white blood cells (T-lymphocytes) in human blood, and also cells of the bone marrow, spleen, liver, and lymph glands. These cells normally manufacture antibodies against disease and cancer. The AIDS patient then has a seriously-impaired immune system and becomes vulnerable to infection by bacteria,

113

protozoa, fungi, and other viruses and malignancies. Death is usually due to one or several other "opportunistic diseases," such as pneumonia, meningitis, tuberculosis, and cancer. The HIV also can directly attack the brain and nervous system, although neurological damage could take years to develop. Such symptoms may occur independent of the typical AIDS symptoms

Is AIDS contagious? How is it spread?

Answer: Although AIDS is contagious, it can't be spread in the same way as the common cold, chicken pox, or measles. Rather it's contagious in the same manner as are sexually transmitted diseases like gonorrhea or syphilis. In fact, research suggests that other sexually transmitted diseases and genital ulcers actually promote the transmission of AIDS. It's thought that these conditions provide an entry route for the HIV or somehow alter the immune system.

After infection with the AIDS virus, some people remain apparently well. Nevertheless, these persons can transmit the virus to others through sexual relations, through sharing needles in intravenous drug use, or when donating blood, organs, tissue, or sperm. AIDS is spread through blood or semen, and possibly through vaginal secretions, although the virus is less concentrated there. During sexual activity, invisible breaks may occur in the skin of the rectum or vagina, allowing passage of the virus. Other *possible* (though far less likely) avenues are the mucous membranes of the eyes, nose, and mouth, which are permeable and thus allow viruses to pass directly into the bloodstream.

The AIDS virus has also been identified in menstrual blood, tears, saliva, sperm, and feces. It's presently considered unlikely that the virus can be transmitted by any means other than sexual contact or by blood exchange.

After studies of families who lived and interacted with AIDS patients, the following is accepted as fact:
* AIDS is not spread by casual contact in school or on the job.
* AIDS is not spread by crying, coughing, sneezing, or by ordinary social kissing. ("French" kissing, or wet kissing, may be an exception.)
* AIDS is not spread by swimming in pools, bathing in hot tubs, or eating in restaurants, even if restaurant workers are carrying the virus.
* AIDS is not spread by shared towels, shared bed linens, or shared eating and drinking utensils.
* AIDS is not spread by mosquito bites, other insects, or pets.
* AIDS is not spread via toilet seats, doorknobs, or telephones.
* The AIDS virus is weak, easily destroyed by standard sterilization measures. Or regular household chlorine bleach, 1 part bleach to 10 parts water, will kill the virus.

114

Now let's look at how it *is* spread.

* AIDS *is* spread by sexual contact: penis-vagina; penis-rectum; mouth-penis; mouth-vagina; mouth-rectum.
* AIDS *is* spread through sharing intravenous needles and syringes such as those used for "shooting" illicit drugs.
* AIDS *is* spread from mother to child. A woman infected with HIV may spread the disease to her developing child during pregnancy, birth, or shortly thereafter. It's also considered possible to transmit the virus through breast-feeding. (Pregnancy can be dangerous for the infected mother. And there's a 15%–50% chance that the baby will be infected before or during birth. Most infants born with AIDS die within months, while carriers may live a few years.)
* AIDS *may be* spread through use of any unsterilized skin-piercing instrument, including needles used for ear piercing or tattooing.
* AIDS *may be* spread via shared razors or toothbrushes, which could use a break in the skin and/or gums to allow passage of the virus directly into the bloodstream. (The only exceptions to the above have been several health workers who somehow came in contact with the blood of AIDS patients through puncture accidents, or by being in a situation where blood squirted into their eyes, mouth, or through breaks in their skin.)

Are some people more likely to contract AIDS?

Answer: Those at high risk are active homosexuals, bisexual individuals, intravenous drug users who use dirty needles and/or who share needles, those who have multiple sex partners, and those who engage in sexual activity with prostitutes. The sexual partners of these people are at risk, too, of course. As someone put it, when you have sexual intercourse with another person you are, in effect, having sex with every person with whom your partner has *ever* had sex.

Although AIDS has been labeled a disease of homosexuals, the number of cases among heterosexuals is increasing. Aside from the women who would be included in the previously-mentioned groups, most of the females who are showing up with AIDS/ARC are wives of infected men. Indeed, males are more likely to transmit the virus to females than vice versa, although the reason is unclear. Scientists are sure that the number of cases among heterosexuals will multiply many times, but they disagree in their projections.

Female prostitutes are a factor in this increase, since most of the "johns" (customers) are heterosexual. Since prostitutes obviously have multiple sex partners, and because many "shoot" intravenous drugs, they're prime targets for the virus. In some large cities up to 50% of the prostitutes tested have been exposed to the AIDS virus and thus can transmit the disease to their unsuspecting customers.

Hemophiliacs and others who received transfusions or plasma prior to March 1985 *may* be at risk. Potential blood donors are screened, and blood is not accepted from high-risk individuals. (It should be noted that because antibodies do not form immediately after exposure to the AIDS virus, a newly-infected person might unknowingly donate blood before a test would read positive. Authorities estimate that less than one in 100,000 donations would fall into this category. Persons facing elective surgery may choose to store up their own blood in advance, to be available if needed.) Donations to blood banks have dropped since the advent of AIDS, presumably out of fear. Be assured that there is *no* danger in donating blood, because one-time, disposable needles are used.

Even individuals who have a negative result on the test for AIDS antibodies could infect others. That's because after exposure to the HIV, antibodies may not show up in a blood test for three to six months, and in some cases, not for up to one year.

What is the test for AIDS?

Answer: Because carriers of the HIV may exhibit no outward symptoms, without a blood test there is *no* way to determine whether an individual has been exposed. Tests are available through personal physicians, community hospitals, and county agencies. These tests do not detect the virus itself, but rather the antibodies produced in response to exposure to the HIV virus.

It seems to me that if one practices safe sex, there's nothing to worry about.

Answer: Current media emphasis centers on "safe sex." But how safe is it, really? Here are some factors to consider.

* Condoms (rubbers) can break, leak, or be used improperly. In pregnancy prevention, condoms are considered to have a 10% or higher failure rate (10 pregnancies out of 100 occasions of sexual intercourse). Yet because of the menstrual cycle a female can become pregnant only a few days of each month. The AIDS/ARC carrier, however, can transmit the virus 365 days of the year.
* The condom *must* be worn from the very beginning (foreplay) until the end of the act of intercourse, since the male typically releases a small amount of semen long before ejaculation.
* The only spermicide shown to be effective at all in repelling the AIDS virus are those containing nonoxynol-9. Researchers make the point, however, that lab test results may differ from actual effectiveness during intercourse.
* It's considered prudent for the female to wear a diaphragm (plus spermicide) *even when* the male wears a condom.

Are you saying that it's impossible to escape AIDS?

Not at all! Individuals are not considered to be at risk *if*:

* Each partner has been absolutely faithful to the other for at least five years. (If either has had intercourse with any other person, both are potentially at risk.)
* Neither partner has used illegal intravenous drugs and/or shared needles during those years.
* Neither partner has had transfusions between 1978 and 1985, when routine screening of blood donors began.

The reassuring news is that although AIDS is often termed a "modern plague," there's an important difference compared to, for example, the black death. AIDS is a *preventable* disease. A spokesman for the Public Health Service says, "AIDS is not a plague that strikes people for no reason, but a disease that strikes people whose behavior allows them to be infected."

Yes, the statistics are frightening, and the projections for the future even more so. Yet it doesn't have to happen. The remedy, however, requires nothing less than a major change in the thinking and practices of our society. Our first task is to be informed. With facts in hand we'll not give in to unreasonable fears.

But information alone is not enough. Adolescents, for example, need more than merely facts. Teens often place themselves at risk because they typically believe (about many things), "It could never happen to me." Teenagers are also subject to peer pressure, and experimentation with sex and drugs is rampant today.

There is a way to be safe! The old virtues, as delineated in the Bible, are the "new" wisdom of our time. Chastity before marriage, absolute faithfulness within marriage, avoiding practices which could be harmful to our own bodies or to other individuals—these are the guidelines laid down by today's health authorities—and by our loving God so very long ago. Medical personnel, Christian or not, would agree that this is the only *truly* "safe sex."

Chancroid

This STD hasn't been much of a factor in the U.S. since the late 1940s. However, in the past few years reported cases have increased sharply, and it is once again being regarded as a significant disease here, as it already is in many parts of the world. Chancroid is a bacterial disease that causes genital ulcers and swollen lymph glands. The usual treatment is sulfonamide drugs, although tetracycline may be used. If not treated, the disease can damage the urinary tract and destroy other body tissue.

Chancroid usually is found among heterosexuals, with three to 25 times more cases among men than women. The higher ratio is in outbreaks involving patrons of prostitutes, probably because just a few women can infect many men, and because the women are hard to locate.

Chlamydia

This is the most prevalent STD in the U.S., especially among young adults ages 17 to 24. It's estimated that each year four million people are affected—40% of them female. (Females on the birth control pill are two to three times more likely to contract chlamydia if exposed.) The infection begins in the urethra and/or the cervix, which then become inflamed. Often it then spreads to the uterus and fallopian tubes, developing into pelvic inflammatory disease (PID), a condition which can result in infertility or sterility. In addition, undetected chlamydia can cause a higher incidence of tubal pregnancies.

It's often difficult to diagnose chlamydia, since 60%–80% of infected females do not display any symptoms for years. Also, typical symptoms—genital inflammation, vaginal discharge, difficulty in urinating, and pain during sexual intercourse—are commonly present in other STDs. Likely symptoms in the male are urinary tract infection (urethritis) plus a discharge from the penis which contains no pus. Untreated males may become sterile. There are now accurate tests to aid in diagnosis. Tetracycline has proven a successful treatment.

Genital Herpes

An estimated 500,000 new cases of genital herpes are reported each year, of which 40% are in females. A viral STD which can be treated but not cured, genital herpes is spread by sexual contact with a person who's experiencing a herpes episode. The blisterlike herpes sores may *not* be present, however. A person can be contagious from the beginning of the time the person feels the very first sensations (prickling, tingling, itching, burning sensation when urinating, watery discharge from the vagina) until the last sore has formed a scab and healed. Experts disagree on whether condoms prevent transmission of herpes. Abstinence during the entire active episode is the only protection.

Within days after the first symptoms, fluid-filled sores appear around the genitals and may last for two to six weeks. Headache, muscle ache, fever, and swollen glands in the groin may accompany or follow the outbreak. During outbreaks sores should be kept clean and dry. Avoid touching active sores, as that can transfer virus particles to other sites on the body or to one's partner. If there are sores in the mouth, using saliva as a wetting agent for contact lenses can transfer the herpes virus to the eyes. Should the virus invade the eye, it can cause lesions on the cornea that may result in partial or complete vision impairment.

Herpes sufferers typically have from one to six outbreaks per year. Triggering factors are individual—anything from emotional stress to wearing clothes that fit too tightly.

There are two special concerns for women. Babies conceived by an infected mother may abort or be born prematurely. Infants can contract the disease during passage through the birth canal of a mother whose herpes is in the active phase. Herpes is life-threatening to these newborns, and many who survive will suffer brain damage or blindness. That makes it essential that the physician carefully monitor the pregnant woman's condition. When herpes is active, delivery of the infant by Caesarean section minimizes the risk for the child.

It's also essential that females have "Pap" smears every six months. Herpes infection is lifelong and greatly multiplies the woman's risk of developing cancer, either of the cervix or of the vulva.

The herpes virus can lie dormant in the body for many years, usually in nerve tissues, without producing symptoms. After the initial infection, it may be reactivated at any point by some triggering event, such as another infection or stress. Close contact with another person who has active genital herpes can produce reinfection or introduce additional virus into the body; an outbreak does not produce immunity.

There is no cure for herpes. Treatment with acyclovir (marketed as Zovirax) reduces the frequency and severity of attacks.

Are there other ways to pick up herpes?

Answer: The proven way is, as described, through sexual intercourse, or through touching the lesions and then touching another site on the body. Medical authorities differ in their opinions as to other means of transmission. For example, the saliva of a herpes sufferer in an active phase may harbor the virus or there could be lesions within the mouth. That would make kissing a means of transmission.

The herpes virus doesn't survive for long outside the body. Research at the UCLA School of Medicine, however, demonstrated that the virus can live for several hours on surfaces and on cloth. So although the virus is killed by normal washing of glasses and cutlery, it seems prudent to avoid sharing them. That would make it wise, also, to forego sharing towels and clothing of the person with active herpes. This information would explain those cases where the herpes patient vows he or she has not engaged in any sexual activity, yet develops genital herpes. Toilet seats are considered safe. Yet it's at least theoretically possible that a person whose genital lesions are "weeping" might leave some serum on the toilet seat that could then contact the skin of the next user. Infection is unlikely, because the amount of drippage would be small. Still, covering the seat with toilet tissue or using a seat cover would offer extra protection.

Genital Warts

The number of cases of genital warts is definitely on the rise, with an estimated one million new victims each year. Genital warts are caused by the human papilloma virus (HPV)—the same virus family responsible for warts on fingers and plantar warts on the soles of feet.

There are great variations in size and appearance. These warts may be white, gray, pink or brown; they may be raised, bumpy, flat, shaped like cauliflower or tiny fingers. Size is usually small—the size of a pencil point to a quarter inch across. Often, however, they're so tiny they can't be seen with the naked eye. There may be two or three together or, sometimes, a cluster which covers a few inches of skin. The cervix is the most likely location, followed by the vagina, vulva, anus, and occasionally, the urethra.

Genital warts are most commonly spread by sexual contact, although researchers aren't quite sure how. (Possibilities for transmission by non-sexual means include contaminated towels, benches, and other surfaces.) Once the causative virus reaches the basal layer of the skin, it may remain dormant for several months. During that time the carrier is not contagious. Then something causes it to work its way back to the upper layers of the skin, and the warts eventually appear.

The real danger in genital warts is that the HPV is also found in nearly all cancers of the lower genital tract, in both male and female (cancers of the cervix, vagina, vulva, and penis). It has been established that not all warts are cancer causing, but there seems to be a definite connection. Researchers believe that several of the strains of the HPV play a part in triggering cancer. Patients, by the way, may be infected with both types of warts and yet be symptom free. "Pap" tests usually provide the first clue of the problem.

Treatment can take several forms: cryotherapy (freezing), laser therapy (vaporizing), or acidic-chemical. The latest treatment for stubborn cases is to inject interferon into or under the warts.

Use of a condom is considered protective against infection. Should there be any sign of infection, have a complete physical.

Gonorrhea (Commonly Called "the Clap")

Annually an estimated 1.8 million people in the U.S. contract gonorrhea. The disease is spread only through sexual contact, and up to 90% of females who have intercourse with an infected male will contract gonorrhea.

For men with gonorrhea the typical symptoms are painful urination and a cloudy, puslike discharge from the penis. Women with gonorrhea may have a cloudy vaginal discharge, possible lower abdominal discomfort, or abnormal vaginal bleeding. Females, too, may find urination painful. However, often *both* males and females have *no* symptoms at all. (If symptoms are to appear, they will do so from two to eight days after infection.) Gonorrhea can also infect the mouth or rectum as a result of oral or anal sexual contact. Typically there are few symptoms.

Left untreated, gonorrhea usually involves a man's entire reproductive tract. Impotence may result. Untreated gonorrhea in the female may infect the uterus and surrounding abdominal area, leading to pelvic inflammatory disease and/or peritonitis. Frequently the end result is sterility. In both sexes, when gonorrhea goes undetected and untreated, it can spread throughout the bloodstream, infecting the joints, bones, tendons, skin, and other parts of the body.

The causative bacteria have become increasingly resistant to antibiotics, although this is still the standard treatment. Use of a condom is considered protective. However, it's important to avoid sexual relations until treatment has cleared up the symptoms, as shown by a follow-up culture.

G. U. Nonspecific (N.S.U.—Nonspecific Urethritis)

This disease attacks the genital-urinary area and is called "non-specific" because researchers have yet to identify the specific causative organism(s). This disease is now considered more rampant than gonorrhea among the general population. Men may display a dripping discharge from the penis (similar to that of gonorrhea) or have a burning sensation upon urination. Women generally have no discharge but may have an inflamed, infected urethra. Treatment is by penicillin or other antibiotic, which does not always effect a cure.

Syphilis

About 98,000 people in the U.S. are infected with syphilis each year; two-thirds of them are male. Syphilis is spread mainly by sexual contact and is highly contagious during the first and second stages. It can, however, be transmitted by kissing, biting, or by a break in the skin coming in contact with an infectious lesion.

This disease is more effectively controlled with antibiotics, although the causative bacteria have shown increasing resistance to drugs. Even when treated, syphilis can erupt many years later. Since it progresses more slowly than gonorrhea, there is time for treatment and for alerting contacts of patients. Within 10 to 40 days—but sometimes as late as three months—after sexual contact with a diseased person, a lesion appears, usually in the anal-genital area. This is a small, red, elevated sore (chancre) that becomes moist and eroded. After four to ten weeks the sore will heal without treatment.

Women may show no symptoms. However, diagnosis can be made by a physical examination and blood test, anytime following the first three weeks after contact. (Before that the tests usually don't reflect the presence of infection.)

Now comes the secondary stage. The internal damage begins, and the diseased person is still contagious. The person may then develop nonitching eruptions or a rash, usually on the trunk of the body, commonly within six weeks to three months. There are other symptoms, usually distinguishable only by a competent physician.

The latent period then arrives, with no symptoms, and the person is not contagious. However, the late stage of syphilis may show itself in any organ—in the brain, the central nervous system, the cardiovascular system, and on the skin. These late effects, which can be disabling, crippling, and disfiguring, may not arrive for more than 30 years.

A pregnant woman infected with syphilis usually transmits the disease to any child conceived during the first two years of the illness. If she is treated during the first four months of pregnancy, the child is generally not infected. The child of such a mother may show signs of congenital syphilis later—up until puberty and even as late as age 30.

By the way, contracting syphilis once and then being treated for it does not confer immunity. A person can be reinfected again and again.

A condom lessens the chance of contracting syphilis. Diaphragms and other contraceptives offer no protection.

Trichomoniasis

Another concern among health officials is the growing incidence of trichomoniasis, caused by a parasite of the vagina in females and of the urethral canal in males. There is no agreement as to how trichomoniasis is contracted. Some authorities consider it strictly a venereal disease because it's easily spread by sexual contact. Others believe it can be contracted in a swimming pool or a bathtub.

The first symptom a woman notices is usually itching and burning, accompanied by a white or yellowish vaginal discharge. There is often inflammation and soreness of the vulva. Susceptibility and severity of symptoms varies among women.

An infected man commonly has no symptoms except for a scant, thin, whitish discharge. Sometimes he will experience itching and burning upon urination. In males the trichomonads may live under the foreskin, may invade the urethral canal, and occasionally the prostrate.

Since husband and wife may pass the disease back and forth for years, it's important to treat both partners simultaneously. (There may also be accompanying bacterial and yeast infection present.) Treatment is by the appropriate prescription drug.

Note: If trichomoniasis and candidiasis (yeast infection) have been ruled out, another type of vaginitis, gardnerella, may be the culprit. This is usually, though not always, spread by sexual contact. A heavy, clear, or grayish discharge with an unpleasant odor is the tip-off. However, a man may carry this infection and never display any symptoms. Antibiotics are the treatment. Repeated infections indicate that both partners should seek medical care simultaneously.

Faced with the appalling statistics on AIDS and sexually transmitted diseases (STD), many of us would like to take our children and go find a nice, safe, deserted island somewhere. Nevertheless, we needn't cower in fear, either for our children or ourselves.

Society is in a mess because of wrong choices that bring unpleasant consequences. The encouraging news is that all of us—at any age—can make *wise* choices that bring *good* results. Kids need to hear that! Even very young children watch TV ads designed to frighten viewers into altering sexual behavior that can lead to death from AIDS.

So it's important to provide a warm, loving atmosphere in which they can voice their fears and ask questions. Use your own judgment as to how detailed your answers will be; you know your own child/children better than anyone. Give enough information to convince them that STD is not to be taken lightly.

When talking with your children, take the positive approach. Remind them (and yourself) that in almost every instance, infection with STD and with AIDS is the result of sexual relations with an infected person, or of using contaminated needles during use of illicit intravenous drugs. These are *avoidable* hazards. Step one is for the individual to *decide* to say no.

Our task as parents, then, is to foster that decisiveness and strength—and self-confidence—in our children. That means speaking frankly about choice-and-consequence, but also frequently reminding them of who they are. The apostle Paul tied it all together and the J. B. Phillips paraphrase sounds especially timely:

> Avoid sexual looseness like the plague! Every other sin that a man commits is done outside his own body, but this is an offense against his own body. Have you forgotten that your body is the temple of the Holy Spirit, who lives in you and is God's gift to you, and that you are not the owner of your own body? You have been bought, and at a price! Therefore bring glory to God in your body.
>
> 1 Corinthians 6:18–20 Phillips

Yet how are Christians to respond when all around us are people who blatantly disregard God's principles for living?

God forgives *all* sin; we know that. We're living with the aftermath of the sexual revolution. What was so highly acclaimed and prized has been revealed for what it is—the grim bondage of health problems that can last for life—or end, too soon, in death.

God forgives—freely, mercifully, unconditionally. The fact that human beings live with the natural consequences of unwise choices doesn't nullify God's forgiveness and acceptance of the repentant sinner. As parents we need to convey this message also—with *love*, not as a threat, not to inspire fear. Choices and actions yield consequences; that's simply the way life is. There is, as they say, no free ride.

Perhaps the trend of public opinion is beginning to turn in that direction. Certainly it's unexpected that "the world" would echo Biblical principles. Yet some experts have summed up their advice in familiar-sounding principles: Say no to drugs and to sex outside the marriage relationship and you are also saying no to AIDS, no to STD, and no to unwanted pregnancy.

But because saying no can be so very difficult, we need to stress something else, too, with our children. As Christians we're not alone in our struggle to withstand the pressures and temptations of living. The "reinforcing rod" in our will is God's Holy Spirit. Paul passes on specific assurance:

> Every test that you have experienced is the kind that normally comes to people. But God keeps his promise, and he will not allow you to be tested beyond your power to remain firm; at the time you are put to the test, he will give you the strength to endure it, and so provide you with a way out.
>
> 1 Corinthians 10:13 TEV

Following God's guidelines, we—and our children—can live in confidence, not fear. Moved by our own absolute forgiveness in Christ, we can accept each other in love, not judgment. And as Christians we can rejoice together in the inspired word of Scripture that remains fresh and up-to-date in every age.

Abortion

My teenager says that abortion is simply "termination of an unwanted pregnancy" and that women have a right to exercise control over their own bodies. I don't agree with her, but how can I counter what she says?

Answer: Legal abortions are widely available. In many states teenagers can obtain a legal abortion without the consent or knowledge of their parents. Community free or low-cost clinics may enable teenagers to obtain such services even though they're financially dependent on their parents.

Medically speaking, abortion is a simple procedure if done within the first trimester (three months) of pregnancy. Some people consider abortion a means of birth control (which it is in many countries) or at least as an alternative if conventional methods fail.

However, abortion is not an option for the Christian. The reason can be found in Psalm 139:13, 15–16:

> You created every part of me; You put me together in my mother's womb . . . When my bones were being formed, carefully put together in my mother's womb, when I was growing there in secret, You knew that I was there—You saw me before I was born (TEV).

This section of Scripture leaves no doubt that the fetus is a human being—with a soul—before birth. Doctors tell us an individual's gender, color of eyes and hair, body build and height, potential intelligence, talents and abilities, and many other characteristics of body and spirit are determined at the moment of conception. Although the fetus is but a half-inch long 28 days after conception, its brain is already growing, its internal ear and eye structures are formed, its heart is formed and beating, and it has a simple digestive system, a functional circulatory system, kidneys, and liver. All this refutes the argument that a fetus is "simply a clump of tissue" or merely "potential life."

Abortion can have a detrimental effect on the future life of the female. Subsequent pregnancies may be seriously affected because there's a greater likelihood of miscarriage or premature delivery. (This effect is intensified when the female is a teenager.) In addition, many women who obtain abortions suffer psychological and emotional trauma, either at the time of the abortion or later, and this may continue for long periods of time.

For Christians and for all serious-minded people, abortion can never be taken lightly. For it is God who has given human beings the ability to become parents—the gift of being partners with Him in the wonder and mystery of new life.

God has given us the privilege and responsibility of caring for our body, but not absolute ownership of it:

> Don't you know that your body is the temple of the Holy Spirit, who lives in you and who was given to you by God? You do not belong to yourselves but to God; He brought you for a price. So use your bodies for God's glory.
> 1 Corinthians 6:19–20 TEV

Nor has God awarded us the power over the life of another human being—not even ourselves:

> It is God who directs the lives of His creatures; every man's life is in His power.
> Job 12:10 TEV

The question of how to deal with an unplanned pregnancy, whether married or single, old or young, is never simple, although prevailing public opinion may make it appear so. As Christians, however, we're *in* the world but not *of* the world. We are "God's own people" (1 Peter 2:9 RSV). Our allegiance—our responsibility—is to God. Thus no matter what may be the situation with which we wrestle, we view it from that perspective:

> For in Him we live, and move, and have our being.
> Acts 17:28 KJV

Homosexuality

What about homosexuality?

Answer: In spite of all the research, there's no unanimous agreement as to the cause(s) of homosexuality. The Bible speaks clearly against homosexual *behavior*. However, it's important to differentiate between condemning homosexual behavior and homosexual persons. As Christians we accept *persons* who have homosexual tendencies, showing them the same love Christ so abundantly showers on all us sinners.

Homosexuality was once a taboo subject but now it is in the news frequently. Today "gays" are portrayed as heroes and heroines of movies, TV shows, and books. Homosexuality is frequently presented as just another choice of life-style, all of them normal and acceptable. Parents are uneasy, fearing that increased exposure of and about homosexuals will somehow lead their children into this life-style. This is seldom true.

Parents may look at a small-boned son and fear he's not a "real male." Or a daughter who lacks the feminine graces, who always showed a preference for typically male activities, may cause her parents to wonder whether there's "something wrong" with her.

Such ideas are stereotypes. For example, adult male homosexuals are in "masculine" fields like engineering, in the professions, in management-level jobs, in professional sports, and in positions of public trust.

Today youngsters are much exposed to the media but have less experience and presumably less mature judgment than adults. Thus they may recall scattered episodes of homosexual play when they were growing up and may question their own sexuality. So it's good to mention casually that such happenings are normal, especially among young boys, and do not indicate latent homosexual tendencies.

Young people need reassurance and acceptance from us, not reinforcement of their own doubts. For instance, we may wonder whether our daughter spends too much time with her girlfriend or whether our son hangs around with the fellows too much. Whether we voice these concerns openly or not, our attitudes will almost surely come through. The message our youngsters will receive is: "I'm not sure you're normal."

So what can a parent do to build a strong self-identity and ensure healthy sexual attitudes?

1. First, last, and most important, we put our major effort into achieving a mutually satisfying, mutually supportive marriage relationship. This gives our children a healthy pattern of male-female interaction. We love each other and our children—and it shows. If we have problems we can't handle, we seek help for the good of our children as well as ourselves.

2. The parent of the other sex tries to be emotionally stable, caring, and loving toward the child.

3. The parent of the same sex is strong but also warm and tender, so the child can have a good relationship and will wish to identify with that parent.

4. We accept our children and their gender. We do not attempt to

make a girl into a substitute boy, or vice versa. Neither do we push them into stereotypes.

5. We accept our children *as they are,* even when they disappoint us in appearance or performance. And we speak our love frequently.

6. We let our children know we're there to help with their problems. We listen to their "sad" stories without laughing or putting them down. We reassure and encourage them every chance we get.

If we follow these principles, our child will feel accepted as a person and will have the confidence to develop healthy relationships.

Premenstrual Syndrome (PMS)

When it's "that time of the month," I'm hard to live with. How do I explain PMS to my teenage daughter?

Answer: PMS won't kill you—but for some women (and their families) this condition makes life extremely unpleasant every month. Symptoms begin 7 to 14 days prior to the menstrual period and usually stop when menstruation begins. Symptoms may include breast swelling and tenderness, nervousness and irritability, headache, fluid retention, increased or decreased sex drive, digestive disturbances, dizziness or fainting, acne outbreaks, and depression.

Severity of symptoms may vary a great deal from one month to the next, and some women are never affected. The cause is fluctuations in the circulating level of hormones (especially estrogen and progesterone) and blood chemicals. These variables increase sodium retention in the bloodstream, which causes edema in body tissue and in the brain. Theories of treatment also vary greatly. Most authorities recommend reducing salt intake and stress. Various vitamins, medications, and/or hormones may be advised.

Toxic Shock Syndrome (TSS)

With the danger of toxic shock, is it safe to use tampons?

Answer: TSS is caused by a strain of staphylococcus bacteria that colonize the vagina and/or uterus and then the bloodstream, releasing a particularly virulent toxin which causes a form of blood poisoning.

Tampon usage, especially of the super-absorbent type, is almost always associated with the disease. This may be because users tend to change such tampons less frequently, thus providing extra time in an environment that allows these bacteria to multiply. However, it should be noted that there have been users of *all* types and brands who have contracted TSS. TSS is a life-threatening illness and requires immediate hospitalization and antibiotics. Initial symptoms are flulike. A beet-red skin rash is characteristic. Kidneys, liver, intestines, stomach, blood, and skin can be affected by the disease.

General recommendations for menstruating females are to avoid the super-absorbent tampons and to change tampons at least every four to six hours. Wash hands before inserting tampons, since the staph bacteria are commonly found on the hands. As an extra precaution, use absorbent pads instead of tampons during the night and maintain cleanliness in the vaginal area.

It's also advisable that diaphragm users *not* leave the diaphragm in place for more than six to eight hours.

THINGS TEENS WONDER ABOUT

Size of Penis

Is a guy's penis ever too big (too small) for the woman?

Answer: Just as people come in all different shapes and sizes, sexual organs do too, and each one is normal for that person. It really doesn't make any difference what size or shape penis a man has; he can still be a satisfying sexual partner for his wife.

As for the woman, the vagina is made to stretch, so it will accommodate any size of penis. This stretching doesn't hurt the wife; it's perfectly normal and the way God made females.

Does a wife enjoy it more if her husband's penis is bigger?

Answer: No, because the sensitive areas of her body are mostly on the outside and in the area around the vaginal opening. Therefore she'll be sexually stimulated just as well if her husband has a smaller penis.

Does it hurt the woman when the man inserts his penis?

Answer: If the female is frightened or nervous or feels guilty, she may tense her muscles all over, including the vaginal opening. When this happens, she may feel some discomfort. Also, when she's feeling this way the lubricating process within the vagina doesn't seem to work as well so the combination of the two may cause some difficulty. That's another reason why intercourse works best within marriage; the couple feels secure and can relax.

Circumcision

Does circumcision make it better for the man?

Answer: So far as authorities can tell, the sensitivity of a man's penis is not affected by circumcision. Nor does it seem to make a difference for the woman. However, it does make it easier to maintain cleanliness. Removal of the foreskin prevents the accumulation of a discharge called smegma, which can develop an objectionable oder.

Intercourse During Menstruation

Will it hurt the woman if a couple has intercourse while she's menstruating?

Answer: There's no physical reason why a couple should not have intercourse during the female's menstrual cycle. It is not painful for her. Each husband and wife must decide for themselves, depending on their own personal feelings.

10. Young Adults: On Their Own

Train up a child in the way he should go; and when he is old, he will not depart from it.

Proverbs 22:6 KJV

Those are reassuring words, and parents down through the ages have clung to them and found them to be true. However, for many young adults there's an interim phase when they seem to turn their backs on everything they've seen and heard in their homes. This is the time of life when our children cut the emotional cords with us and strike out on their own, often living by values with which we disagree. During this period many a parent wonders, "Where did I go wrong?"

Some psychologists say this breaking-away stage is a necessary step in the development of the self-functioning adult. It can be a period of distress for both parent and child. Parents see all the years invested in raising their young people—who were and probably still are the central focus of their own lives—and wonder what is left. All too often the parent panics and attempts to hang on desperately.

This practice can take many forms. Some parents refuse outright to let a child go away to college, for instance. "I had my heart set on going to a school 100 miles from home," said Kristen, "but Mom and Dad said they thought it 'best' that I live at home and go to the junior college. Who did they think they were kidding, anyway? I knew the real reason. If they'd been honest they'd have admitted they just couldn't stand to see me leave home. I should think they'd be glad to get me out of their hair and be alone for a change.

"I guess if I were really a good daughter I'd want to live at home, but the truth is I resent being forced to stay and I get out of the house at every opportunity. I just want a chance to be on my own. Is that so wrong? Yet when I start talking about it Mom goes off to bed with one of her sick headaches and Dad gets all misty-eyed. Then I feel so guilty I just give up. I guess I'll be here till I'm 35!"

Such manipulation is often unconscious on the part of the parent; we all tell ourselves, "It's for their own good!" and we can find a dozen reasons to prove it. But underneath we fear being alone, dread change, feel anxious that the new stage of life which looms ahead may be an empty one.

A RIGHT TO THEIR OWN LIVES

It's well to remind ourselves again that we don't "own" our children. They're people in their own right, with the obligation and privilege to make decisions and solve problems for themselves. (However, if we note actions we know to be without doubt against God's will, we have a duty to speak as one concerned Christian to another.)

"When my daughter became an adult, I didn't know how I should talk with her," said Rachel. "For awhile I just skirted around issues that bothered me—figured it was none of my business now. But I began to realize we're still united in Christ, so I 'rushed in where angels fear to tread,' as they say, afraid Kelly would get angry.

"I managed to stay low-key. Used lots of 'I messages'—like 'I'm really concerned because I'm afraid you'll be hurt' or 'I'm uneasy because I wonder if you've thought about how that stacks up against Christian values.'

"Once in awhile I slipped up and started the old line: 'Kelly, you should . . . ,' but I'd catch myself and start over," said Rachel, smiling. "Actually, these turned out to be some of the best talks we've ever had! Although Kelly didn't seem too impressed at the time, she made some changes later that showed she didn't just resist my viewpoint out of hand."

Rachel learned a valuable lesson for Christian parents. Relating to grown children is most effective—and most harmonious—when we accept and respect our young people. We can still be their valued friends, still listen, still offer occasional counsel, but as adult-to-adult.

Our active parenting is over. Future shaping will come mostly from God and the sometimes-painful experiences of living.

THEY'RE LIVING TOGETHER!

One prospect that today's parents dread is that of a young couple living together without benefit of marriage. Television and movies to the contrary, surveys show the trend to this life-style is not really overwhelming. However, when it occurs most parents find it extremely difficult to handle.

"When Callie moved in with Toby, I thought I'd die," said Annette. "I just couldn't accept it. I know and she knows that God's Word speaks against sex outside of marriage. Wick and I have always had a happy marriage, always told our kids there's nothing better, that it's worth waiting for. We thought they agreed with us. Then Callie went off to school, and the next thing we knew she was living with Toby.

"It's been months, yet I still lie there in the middle of the night and think about all my failures as a parent. It seems all my thoughts begin with 'If only . . .' I can't get it out of my mind. I just know she's ruining her life! And how will she pick up the pieces after this affair breaks up? What if she gets pregnant? Wick and I never thought a child of ours would be living in sin, and we're not coping very well. I just don't know what got into that girl. . . ."

Most of us would have many of the same feelings. Although the situation itself troubles us, the openness, the fact that such couples seem almost to flaunt their relationship, troubles us even more.

If we're honest we'll admit there's another factor too. We're embarrassed. "What will people say?" we wonder. "What kind of parent will they think I've been? How shall I handle this situation?"

Over and over we rehash our dilemma, wondering what course of action is best. In the end we have no real choice but to accept the fact that these young adults are accountable for their own actions. They must live with the results of their decision, good or bad.

This doesn't mean we remain silent. Rather, as adult Christians we'll speak the truth in love. We'll be honest about our feelings (the "I messages" again). For if we try to cover them, pretend they don't exist, our child—who knows us so well—will sense them anyhow.

On the other hand, belaboring our objections is counterproductive, for if we lay down conditions, if we force our child to make a choice between us and the "live-in," we may put up walls that last for years. Whether we like it or not, the fact is that we can't *force* our adult child to adopt our own Christian values system. But we can continue to pray for him/her—and continue to demonstrate our love and caring, standing by to help and to give counsel if asked.

We can forgive ourselves, too, for our failures as parents. All of us have made mistakes, of course, and would be far wiser parents the second time around. But there is no second time. We did the best we could with the wisdom and maturity we had. It serves no purpose, either for us or our children, to dwell on what we should have done. Rather we can rest on our gracious God's promise to use even our blunders and omissions for good (Romans 8:28).

AND THEN THEY WERE MARRIED...

When a child marries, parents often breathe a sigh of relief. Even if there are doubts about a prospective child-in-law, they may well feel that marriage is preferable to living together or possible unwed pregnancy. Now the young adult is establishing a legal, separate family unit. Society, the church, and we ourselves pronounce our blessing.

But we may not yet be ready to give up control of our children, to let them function as adults whose major commitment must be to their marriage. Millie, for instance, feels she has the right to walk into her son's home unannounced. "Why not?" she says. "Royce is still my child! Why should I have to telephone first? And why bother to knock when I have a key? After all, I'm not a stranger—I'm family!"

But her daughter-in-law doesn't see it quite that way. "We never know when that door is going to open," says Renee. "This is our home, but we have no privacy. And she expects us to spend every Sunday afternoon at her house. Honestly, Royce's mom must think she owns us! I know she means well, but we have our own lives to live.

"And she asks the most intimate questions—inquires about our 'adjustment,' and are we 'having any problems.' We know what she means, of course, but I'll be hanged if I'm going to discuss our sex life with her. And boy! do we feel the pressure about having a baby!"

No couple should feel it's their "duty" to supply their parents with grandchildren. This has to be a decision a couple reaches because *they* sincerely want children. We may dream of becoming grandparents, feel a marriage isn't a marriage without children. But our own children are the ones who will face the very real demands of parenthood.

If and when they do become parents, we'll want to respect our children's rights as parents. The way they choose to bring up their children is up to them.

IT'S THEIR DECISION

In short, the whole subject of relating to grown children, married or unmarried, could largely be summed up in three words: It's their decision. Hard to accept, isn't it? Yet that's exactly what we wished for ourselves—the freedom to run our own lives, to make our own choices, to be respected as adults.

Our relationship with our grown children is a fragile thing, like holding a tiny bird in our hand. If we hold too tightly, it will die. But if we treat this living thing kindly and show love, if we set it free to follow its own leading and fly its own journey, it will come back of its own free will. Then we'll have a friend for life—one who *chooses* to have a relationship with us.

Surely such friendship must be the best possible reward for all the years of parenting!

Epilog

Perhaps after reading this book you feel that you haven't talked to your children enough, haven't been open enough. You may even feel you have damaged your youngster's sexual attitudes for life.

What can you—what can all of us—do?

First of all, let's be kind to ourselves and forgive ourselves for our very human failures. After all, we're products of our own upbringing, of the hang-ups of our parents, after whom we patterned our own parenting. Most of us feel very open by comparison. And we probably are!

So we begin where we are, whatever our children's ages. Should they be younger, we can simply fill in what we've omitted and pick up from there. If they're teenagers or older, we'll want to openly admit our failures and do what we can to reopen the door to communication. Forgiveness and acceptance can flow between us, even now.

But then we put it behind us. We all survived our less-than-perfect parenting, and our children will too. If we have had a loving relationship with our spouse and/or have served as a good role model, we've already done the most important thing.

Still, what if we feel we've failed even at that?

Then we do what God has told us to do with all our cares. We cast them upon Him and leave them there. We rest in the certainty that Christ totally paid for these sins, too, when He died on the cross and rose again. We trust His grace and power and love to transform our failures into good in the lives of our children—in His way, in His own good time. We accept our children and ourselves as fellow redeemed sinners.

And then we move on to the next phase of living, forgiven and free to be the best man or woman we can be, enjoying our own sexuality. For at any age we are sexual beings.

God planned it that way.

And as He said when He created the first male and female:
Behold, it is very good!

Glossary

Abortion
(a-BOR-shun)

The premature termination of a pregnancy.
There are three types:
Voluntary. A procedure performed at the request of the pregnant woman;
Spontaneous (miscarriage). A natural termination usually due to some abnormal development of the fetus;
Therapeutic. A medically recommended procedure prompted by abnormal developments that threaten the mother's life or the fetus.
Some common methods of induced abortion include the following:
D & C (Dilatation & Curettage). A medical procedure in which the cervix is dilated and a spoon-shaped surgical instrument called a curette is used to scrape the lining of the uterus. Used during the first 12 weeks of pregnancy.
Hysterotomy. A major surgical procedure in which the fetus is removed through an incision in the abdomen. Used only after 12th week of pregnancy.
Menstrual extraction (regulation). Extracting the lining of the uterus (normally part of the menstrual process) by a suction technique; normally done within two weeks after a missed menstrual period, before positive diagnosis of pregnancy can be made.
Morning-after pill. Prescription drug taken by the woman in single dosage, after sexual intercourse to prevent implantation of fertilized egg.
Saline abortion. Injection of saline (salt) solution into uterus, causing abortion to occur spontaneously. Used only after 14th week of pregnancy.
Vacuum curettage. After dilation of the cervix, suction is used to empty the uterus. Can be used up to the 12th week of pregnancy.

Abstinence
(AB-stuh-nunce)

To voluntarily avoid: In sexual connotation, to refrain from sexual intercourse.

Acne
(AK-nee)

A condition of the complexion, characterized by pimples, blackheads, and/or excess oiliness. Common in adolescents.

Adolescence
(a-doh-LES-sens)

The period of life between puberty and adulthood.

Adultery
(a-DULL-ter-ee)

Sexual intercourse with a person who is legally married to someone else. The term is often used to describe any sexual intercourse outside of marriage.

Afterbirth

See Placenta.

AIDS

(Acquired Immune Deficiency Syndrome) Life-threatening viral disease. Transmitted through exchange of blood and/or semen, either by sexual contact or by use of dirty needles in use of illicit intravenous drugs. May also be the result of receiving transfusion of contaminated blood products.

Amniocentesis
(am-nee-o-sen-TEE-sis)

A procedure whereby a sample of the amniotic fluid surrounding the fetus is drawn and analyzed to detect possible birth defects.

Amnion
(AM-nee-on)

The thin membrance which forms the sac of water surrounding the fetus within the uterus. Contains amniotic fluid, in which the fetus is immersed for protection against shocks and jolts.

Anal Sex
(AY-nal)

Sexual relations where penis is inserted into the rectum.

Androgen
(AN-dro-jen)

A hormone which influences growth and the sex drive in the male. Produces masculine secondary sex characteristics (voice changes, hair growth, etc.)

Anus
(AY-nuss)

The opening at the base of the buttocks through which solid waste is eliminated from the intestines.

ARC

(Aids Related Complex) Presence of antibodies to the AIDS virus, but person does not exhibit AIDS disease.

Areola
(a-REE-o-la)

The dark tissue area around the nipple of the female breast.

Artificial Insemination

The medical procedure of injecting semen into the vagina close to the cervix by artificial means. It can enable pregnancy in spite of fertility problems.

Birth Canal

See Vagina.

Birth Control

Technically, the control/prevention of a birth, regardless of method. Commonly used term referring to contraception and/or contraceptive methods (the prevention of conception by use of devices, drugs, or other means).

Birth Control Pill

See Contraception.

Bisexual
(by-SECK-shoo-al)

Having both male and female sex organs. Commonly used term for describing a sexual interest in both sexes.

Bladder
(BLAD-er)

A sac in the pelvic region where urine is stored until elimination.

Breech Birth

The birth position when the baby's feet or buttocks appear first instead of the usual (headfirst) position.

Caesarean Section
(si-SAIR-ee-an)

(Caesarean Birth; "C" Section)
Delivery of a baby by surgical incision through the abdomen into the uterus.

Candidiasis
(can-dih-DYE-a-sis)

Form of vaginitis caused by yeast-type fungus (*candida albicans*). Commonly referred to as a "yeast infection."

Castration
(kas-TRAY-shun)

Removal of the sex glands—the testicles in men, the ovaries in women.

Cervix
(SER-vicks)

The narrow, lower part of the uterus, which opens into the deep portion of the vagina.

Chancre (SHANG-ker)	A small sore or ulcerated area, usually on the genitals, which is the first symptom of syphilis.
Chancroid (SHAN-kroyd)	Sexually transmitted bacterial disease. Causes genital ulcers and swollen lymph glands. If left untreated, can damage urinary tract and destroy other tissue.
Change of Life	*See* Climacteric; Menopause.
Chastity (CHAS-ti-tee)	Abstention from illicit sexual intercourse.
Chromosome (KRO-mo-soam)	One of the more or less rodlike bodies found in the nucleus of all cells, containing the heredity factors or genes. 22 pairs of chromosomes account for a person's hereditary characteristics. The 23rd pair determines sex. *See* X Chromosome and Y Chromosome.
Circumcision (ser-kum-SIZH-un)	Surgical removal of the foreskin or prepuce of the penis. Originally a Jewish rite performed as a sign of reception into their faith; now generally performed for purposes of cleanliness.
Climacteric (kly-MACK-ter-ik)	The time of physical and emotional change—the end of a menstruation in women and a lessening of sex-hormone production in both sexes. *See* Menopause and Midlife Crisis.
Climax	*See* Orgasm.
Clitoris (KLIT-or-iss)	A small, highly sensitive female organ located just above the urethra.
Coitus (KO-ih-tus)	Sexual intercourse between male and female, in which the penis is inserted into the vagina.
Colostrum (ko-LAH-strum)	The nourishing, thin, milky fluid secreted by a woman's breasts just before and after she gives birth. Characterized by high protein content thought to contribute to the child's early immunity from infectious disease.
Conception (kon-SEP-shun)	(Impregnation) Penetration of the ovum (female egg cell) by a sperm, resulting in development of an embryo—new life.
Condom	*See* Contraception.
Congenital (kon-JEN-i-tal)	Existing from birth. May or may not be inherited.
Conjugal (KON-jew-gal)	Pertaining to marriage, i.e., conjugal love.
Continence (KON-ti-nens)	Exercising self-restraint, particularly regarding the sex drive.
Contraception (kon-trah-SEP-shun)	(Birth control) The prevention of conception by use of devices, drugs, or other means. Commomly used methods include the following: *Birth control pill.* A contraceptive drug made of synthetic hormones that prevent ovulation. Available only on prescription and must be taken as prescribed. *Cervical caps* (SER-vih-kal). Prescription item, barrier

method of contraception, fits over cervix. Long used in Europe, under trial in U.S. Similar effectiveness to diaphragm, but said to be less irritating and can be left in place for longer period.

Condom (KON-dum). A thin rubber sheath placed over the erect penis before intercourse to prevent the sperm from entering the vagina.

Contraceptive sponge. Nonprescription, disposable, polyurethane sponge, two inches in diameter, fits over cervix. Comes presaturated with spermicide (nonoxynol 9), which is activated when moistened with water, prior to insertion. Effective for 24 hours, including multiple acts of intercourse. Very slight risk of toxic shock syndrome.

Diaphragm (DIE-a-fram). A thin rubber disc which covers the cervix and prevents sperm from entering the uterus. Must be individually fitted by a doctor.

Premature withdrawal. Withdrawal of the penis from the vagina before ejaculation. Largely unreliable because of possible release of sperm before ejaculation.

Rhythm method. Abstinence from intercourse during the woman's fertile days as determined by her menstrual cycle.

Vaginal foam, jelly, suppositories, etc. Non-prescription products for the female which are applied within the vagina. Most contain a spermicide—chemical substance which destroys sperm cells.

Copulation	*See* Coitus.
Cowper's Glands (KOO-perz)	Two small glands, one on each side of the male urethra, which secrete a part of the seminal fluid.
Cunnilingus (kun-i-LING-us)	The act of applying the mouth or tongue to the vulva, to stimulate the female.
D & C	(Dilatation & Curettage) A medical procedure in which the cervix is dilated and a spoon-shaped medical instrument called a curette is used to scrape the lining of the uterus.
Delivery	The process of giving birth.
Douche (doosh)	The cleaning of the vagina with a stream of liquid solution or water.
Dysfunction, Sexual	*See* Sexual Dysfunction.
Dysmenorrhea (dis-men-o-REE-ah)	Painful menstruation.
Ectopic Pregnancy (ek-TOP-ik)	An abnormal pregnancy in which the fetus develops outside the uterus.
Ejaculation (ee-jack-yoo-LAY-shun)	The discharge of semen from the penis.
Embryo (EM-bree-oh)	The unborn in its earliest stages of development. In humans, the fertilized ovum during the first eight weeks of its growth.

Endometriosis (en-doe-mee-tree-OH-sis)	Condition in which bits of uterine lining (*endometrium*) become implanted outside the uterus—in the abdominal cavity, on ovaries, and/or on fallopian tubes. A major cause of infertility. Cause remains unknown.
Endometrium (en-doe-MEE-tree-um)	The lining of the uterus, which thickens and fills with blood in preparation for a fertilized ovum.
Epididymis (ee-pi-DID-i-miss)	The mass of tiny coils connecting the testicles with the sperm duct.
Episiotomy (ee-pee-zee-AH-toh-mee)	An incision made in the vaginal entrance during delivery to facilitate the birth of a child.
Erection (ee-RECK-shun)	The enlargement and hardening of the penis or clitoris as tissues fill with blood, usually during sexual excitement.
Erogenous Zone (ee-RAH-jen-us)	Any area of the body that is sexually sensitive or stimulating such as mouth, lips, breast, nipples, and genitals.
Erotic (ee-RAH-tik)	Sexually stimulating.
Estrogen (ESS-tro-jen)	A hormone which affects functioning of the menstrual cycle and produces female secondary sex characteristics (breast development, widened hips, etc.)
Eunuch (YOO-nuck)	A castrated male.
Exhibitionist (ex-i-BISH-un-ist)	A person who compulsively exposes his/her sex organs in public.
Extramarital (ex-tra-MARE-i-tal)	"Outside of marriage"; often used to refer to illicit sexual intercourse, i.e., "extramarital affair."
Fallopian Tube (fa-LOW-pee-an)	The tube through which the egg passes from each ovary to the uterus.
Fellatio (fuh-LAY-shee-o)	The act of applying the mouth or tongue to the penis to stimulate the male.
Fertility	The ability to reproduce.
Fertilization	Penetration of the female ovum by a single sperm, resulting in conception.
Fetus (FEE-tuss)	The unborn child from the third month after conception until birth.
Follicle, Ovarian (FAH-lih-kull, o-VAIR-ee-an)	The small sac near the surface of the ovary which holds the developing egg cell (ovum).
Foreplay	The beginning stage of sexual intercourse, during which partners may kiss, caress, and touch each other in order to achieve full sexual arousal.
Foreskin	The loose skin covering the tip of the penis, removed during circumcision. Also called the prepuce (PREE-puce).

Fornication (for-ni-KAY-shun)	Sexual intercourse between unmarried men and women.
Frigidity (fri-JID-i-tee)	Commonly used term for the sexual dysfunction in which a woman is unable to respond to sexual stimulation.
Gene (jean)	The carrier for hereditary traits in chromosomes.
Genital Herpes	*See* Venereal Disease.
Genitalia (jen-i-TAIL-ya)	(Genitals; Genital Organs) Visible reproductive or sex organs. Usually denotes vagina, vulva, and clitoris in females and the penis and testicles in males.
Gestation (jes-TAY-shun)	The period from conception to birth, approximately nine months.
Glans (glanz)	The head of the penis, exposed when the foreskin is pushed back, or after circumcision.
Gonads (GO-nads)	Sex glands—testicles (male), ovaries (female).
Gonorrhea (gon-er-EE-uh)	*See* Venereal Disease.
G.U. Nonspecific	*See* Venereal Disease.
Gynecologist (guy-na-KOLL-o-jist)	A physician who specializes in the treatment of female sexual and reproductive organs.
Heredity (her-ED-it-ee)	Traits, characteristics, or diseases transmitted from parents to children.
Hermaphrodite (her-MAF-ro-dite)	An individual born with both male and female sex organs.
Heterosexual (het-er-o-SECK-shoo-al)	One who is sexually attracted to or sexually active with persons of the other sex.
Homosexual (ho-mo-SECK-shoo-al)	One who is sexually attracted to or sexually active with persons of one's own sex.
Hormone (HOR-moan)	A chemical substance, produced by an endocrine gland, which has a particular effect on the function of other organs in the body.
Hymen (HIGH-men)	A thin membrane which partially closes the entrance to the vagina. Sometimes called the maidenhead.
Hysterectomy (hiss-ter-ECK-to-mee)	Surgical removal of the uterus.
Hysterotomy (hiss-ter-OT-o-mee)	*See* Abortion.
Impotence (IM-po-tens)	A type of male sexual dysfunction; inability to achieve or maintain erection of the penis during sexual intercourse.
Incest (IN-sest)	Sexual intercourse between close relatives such as father and daughter, mother and son, or brother and sister.

Infertility (in-fer-TILL-ih-tee)	Diagnosis arrived at when both husband and wife are healthy and wife does not conceive after one year of sexual intercourse unprotected by contraceptives. (For females who've been on the birth control pill, an extra three months is added to that baseline period.)
Intercourse, Sexual	*See* Coitus.
Intra-Uterine Device, *IUD* (in-trah-YOU-ter-in)	A small metal or plastic device inserted into the uterus by a physician and left in place. Abortive in character, in that it is thought to prevent a fertilized ovum from being implanted in the uterus and continuing its development. According to a study reported in the *Journal of the American Medical Association,* users are up to nine times more likely to develop pelvic inflammatory disease, which can result in later tubal pregnancy, or even sterility.
In-Vitro Fertilization (in-VEE-trow fer-till-ih-ZAY-shun)	Process whereby the egg is removed from the female's fallopian tube(s), fertilized with male sperm in the laboratory, and then implanted into the uterus. (Either egg or sperm may have been frozen for storage.)
IUD	*See* Intra-Uterine Device.
Jock Itch	A fungus infection causing irritation in the genital area.
Labor	The birth stage in which the cervix gradually dilates, allowing strong contractions of the uterine muscles to push the baby through the vagina and out of the mother's body.
Lactation (lak-TAY-shun)	The production and secretion of milk by the mammary glands in the mother's breasts, following childbirth. The process continues so long as she nurses her child.
Lesbian (LEZ-be-an)	A female homosexual.
Libido	*See* Sex Drive.
Maidenhead	*See* Hymen.
Masochism (MASS-o-kiz-um)	Cruelty to self; receiving sexual pleasure from having pain inflicted or by being harshly dominated.
Masturbation (mass-ter-BAY-shun)	Self-stimulation of one's sex organs, often to the point of orgasm.
Menarche (me-NAR-kee)	The onset of the menstrual cycle in a girl.
Menopause (MEN-o-pawz)	(Change of Life; Climacteric) The end of menstruation in women, usually between the ages of 45 and 55.
Menstruation (men-stroo-AY-shun)	The discharge through the vagina of blood from the uterus. This menstrual "period" usually occurs every 28–30 days in females, between puberty and menopause.
Midlife Crisis	Current term for the change of life (climacteric) in men, usually between ages 50 and 60; sometimes called male menopause. May evoke feelings of restlessness and failure.
Midwife	Person capable of caring for woman's gynecological needs

143

and aiding in delivery of infants. Usually a female nurse with additional medical training who has been certified and has passed the individual state's requirements. (This may not be true of all.) Many work with obstetricians. Legal status varies from state to state.

Miscarriage

(Spontaneous Abortion) The natural expulsion of the fetus from the uterus, before it is mature enough to live, usually due to some abnormal development.

Monilia
(mon-ILL-yah)

(Yeast Infection) A yeastlike fungus which invades the vagina, causing itching and inflammation. Not a venereal disease. Often a result of vaginal douching or antibiotics.

Narcissism
(NAR-sis-izm)

Excessive love of self; egotism; sexual desire or admiration for one's own body.

Nocturnal Emission
(nok-TER-nal
ee-MISH-un)

(Wet Dream) Involuntary male erection and ejaculation during sleep.

Nymphomaniac
(nim-foe-MAY-nee-ack)

A female who experiences excessive sexual desire.

Obstetrician
(ob-ste-TRISH-un)

A physician who specializes in the care of women during pregnancy, childbirth, and immediately thereafter.

Oral Sex

See Cunnilingus; Fellatio.

Orgasm
(OR-gaz-um)

(Climax) The peak of excitement in sexual activity.

Ovaries
(OH-va-rees)

The two female sex glands found on either side of the uterus, in which the ova (egg cells) are formed. They also produce hormones which influence female body characteristics.

Ovulation
(av-yoo-LAY-shun)

Release of the mature (ripe) ovum from the ovary to the fallopian tube.

Ovum
(OH-vum)

(Plural: ova) Female reproductive cell (egg) found in the ovary. After fertilization by a sperm, the human egg develops into an embryo and then a fetus.

Penis
(PEE-nis)

Male sex organ through which semen is discharged and urine is passed.

PID

(Pelvic Inflammatory Disease) Infection involving female reproductive organs. Often leaves permanent damage resulting in later tubal pregnancies, infertility, and/or sterility. Often linked with untreated STD or use of the IUD.

Pituitary
(pih-TOO-i-tair-ee)

A gland at the base of the brain which controls functions of all the other ductless glands, especially sex glands, adrenals, and thyroid.

Placenta
(pluh-SENT-uh)

The spongelike organ that connects the fetus to the lining of the uterus by means of the umbilical cord. It serves to feed the fetus and to dispose of waste. Expelled from the uterus after the birth of a child (afterbirth).

PMS

(Premenstrual Syndrome) Discomfort felt by some females for 7 to 14 days prior to menstrual period. Caused by fluctuations in hormone levels.

Pornography
(por-NOG-raf-ee)

Literature, motion pictures, art, or other means of expression which, without any concern for personal or moral values, intend simply to be sexually arousing.

Postpartum
(post-PAR-tum)

Following childbirth.

Pregnancy
(PREG-nan-cee)

Period from conception to birth; the condition of having a developing embryo or fetus within the female body.

Premature Ejaculation
(ee-jack-yoo-LAY-shun)

A form of sexual dysfunction in which the man ejaculates before, while, or just after inserting the penis into the vagina.

Prenatal
(pree-NAY-tal)

Before birth.

Prepuce
(PREE-puce)

See Foreskin.

Progesterone
(pro-JES-ter-own)

(Progestin) The female "pregnancy hormone" which prepares the uterus to receive the fertilized ovum.

Promiscuous
(pro-MISS-kyoo-us)

Engaging in sexual intercourse with many persons; engaging in casual sexual relationships.

Prophylactic
(prah-fil-LAK-tik)

A device or drug used to prevent disease, often specifically venereal disease. Common term for the condom.

Prostate
(PRAH-state)

Male gland which surrounds the urethra and neck of the bladder and secretes part of the seminal fluid.

Prostitute
(PRAH-sti-toot)

An individual who engages in sexual activity for money.

Puberty
(PYOO-ber-tee)

The period of rapid development that marks the end of childhood; sex organs mature and produce either ovaries or sperm; the girl becomes a young woman and the boy a young man.

Pubic
(PYOO-bik)

Regarding the lower part of the abdominal area, where hair grows in a triangular patch.

Rape
(rayp)

Forcible sexual intercourse with a person who does not consent.

Rectum
(RECK-tum)

The lower end of the large intestine, ending at the anus.

Rhythm Method

See Contraception.

Sadism
(SAD-iz-um)

Cruelty; receiving sexual pleasure by inflicting pain on the sexual partner.

Safe Period

The interval in the menstrual cycle when the female is presumably not ovulating and therefore unable to become pregnant.

Scrotum
(SKRO-tum)

The sac of skin suspended between the male's legs that contains the testicles.

Semen (SEE-men)	(Seminal Fluid; Seminal Emission) The fluid made up of sperm, secretions from the seminal vesicles, prostate and Cowper's glands, and the epididymis. Ejaculated through the penis when the male reaches orgasm.
Seminal Vesicles (SEM-i-nal VESS-i-cals)	Two storage pouches for sperm (which is produced in the testicles). Located on either side of the prostate, they are attached to and open into the sperm ducts.
Sex Drive	(Libido: li-BEE-doe) The desire for sexual activity.
Sex, Oral	*See* Cunnilingus; Fellatio.
Sex Organs	Commonly refers to the male's penis and female's vagina.
Sexual Dysfunction	General term covering problems in sexual performance.
Sexual Intercourse	*See* Coitus.
Smegma (SMEG-mah)	A thick accumulation of secretions under the foreskin of the penis or around the clitoris; has an unpleasant odor.
Sodomy (SAH-dah-mee)	Any of a variety of sexual behaviors, broadly defined by law as deviant, such as sexual intercourse by humans with animals, mouth-genital contact, or anal intercourse between human beings.
Sperm	The male reproductive cell(s), produced in the testicles, having the capacity to fertilize the female ova, resulting in pregnancy.
Sperm Bank	A storage facility for donor sperm that is used in artificial insemination.
Spermatic Duct (sper-MAT-ik)	(Vas Deferens) The tube in the male through which sperm passes from the epididymis to the seminal vesicles and urethra.
Spermatic Cord	The tube in the male by which the testicle is suspended; contains the sperm ducts, veins, and nerves.
Spermicide	*See* Contraception.
Spontaneous Abortion	*See* Miscarriage.
STD	(Sexually Transmitted Disease) More precise term for venereal disease.
Sterility (ster-ILL-it-ee)	The inability to reproduce.
Sterilization (ster-ill-ih-ZAY-shun)	A procedure by which a male or female is rendered unable to produce children, but can still engage in sexual intercourse. The following are some of the most common surgical methods: *Laparoscopy* (la-pa-ROS-ko-pee). Tiny incisions in the abdomen, through which the fallopian tubes are cut or cauterized. Also called "Band-Aid Sterilization." *Tubal ligation/Occlusion* (too-bul-lie-GAY-shun/oh-KLEW-zuhn). Procedures that cut or seal the fallopian tubes to prevent passage of eggs from ovaries into area where fertilization usually occurs. Technique may be via laparoscopy, posterior colpotomy (approach through the

	rear of the vagina), or through a minilaparotomy (incision just above the line of pubic hair). *Sometimes* reversible. *Vasectomy* (vuh-SECK-toe-mee). The male sperm-carrying duct is cut, part is removed, and the ends tied.
Surrogate Mother (SER-ah-gate)	A woman who agrees to become pregnant through artificial insemination (often for a fee) and to carry the fetus to term for an infertile couple. The sperm is usually that of the husband.
Syphilis	*See* Venereal Disease.
Testes (TES-teez)	(Testicles) The two male sex glands which produce sperm, suspended within a sac of skin between the legs.
Testosterone (tes-TOSS-ter-own)	Male sex hormone produced by the testes; causes and maintains male secondary sex characteristics (voice change, hair growth, etc.)
Transgenderist (trans-JEN-der-ist)	A person who identifies very strongly with the other sex and may dress in the clothing of that sex.
Transsexual (trans-SECK-shoo-al)	One who feels psychologically like a member of the other sex and is willing to undergo "sex change" surgery to achieve the outward appearance of the other sex.
Transvestite	One who has a compulsion to dress in the clothing of the other sex.
Trichomoniasis (trick-uh-muh-NY-uh-sis)	*See* Venereal Disease.
Trimester (TRY-mes-ter)	A period of three months. The nine months of pregnancy are usually divided into trimesters.
TSS	(Toxic Shock Syndrome) Life-threatening bacterial disease, much more common in females. Initial symptoms are flulike with beet-red skin rash. Most often linked to use of super-absorbent tampons and/or failure to change tampons frequently.
Twins	*Fraternal twins:* Two children, developed from two separate ova, fertilized by two separate sperm, usually at the same time. *Identical twins:* Two children, developed from a single ovum, fertilized by a single sperm.
Umbilical Cord (uhm-BILL-ih-kal)	The cord connecting the fetus to the placenta, through which the fetus receives nourishment.
Urethra (yoo-REE-thra)	The duct through which urine passes from the bladder and is eliminated from the body.
Urine (YOO-rin)	The body's liquid waste, manufactured by the kidneys from waste materials in the blood, stored in the bladder, and eliminated through the urethra.
Urologist (yoo-RAHL-i-jist)	A physician who specializes in treating urinary tract problems of both sexes, as well as the genital tract of males.

Uterus (YOO-ter-us)	(Womb: WOOM) The small, muscular, pear-shaped female organ in which the fetus develops; has the ability to accommodate the growing child (children).
Vagina (vuh-JY-na)	(Birth Canal) The canal in the female body between the uterus and the vulva; receives the penis during intercourse; the canal through which an infant passes at birth.
Vasectomy	*See* Sterilization.
Venereal Disease (ven-EAR-ee-al)	(VD) Any of a variety of contagious diseases contracted almost entirely by sexual intercourse. Some of the most common are AIDS, chancroid, chlamydia, genital herpes, genital warts, gonorrhea, G.U. Nonspecific, trichomoniasis, and syphilis.
Virgin (VER-jin)	A person who has never had sexual intercourse.
Vulva (VUL-va)	The female's external sex organs, including the *Labia majora* and *Labia minora*, the outer and inner folds of skin (lips) surrounding the vagina and the clitoris.
Wasserman Test	A blood test to determine present or past infection with syphilis.
Wet Dream	*See* Nocturnal Emission.
Withdrawal	*See* Contraception.
Womb	*See* Uterus.
X Chromosome	A chromosome which determines sex, present in all female ova and in one-half of a male's sperm. If the egg is fertilized by a sperm having an X chromosome, a female will be conceived (XX).
Y Chromosome	A sex-determining chromosome present in one-half of a male's sperm. If an ovum is fertilized by a sperm with a Y chromosome, a male will be conceived (XY).
Zygote (ZY-goat)	The single cell which results from union of the sperm and egg at conception. Another term for the fertilized egg.

Index

T

U

V

W